RACISM

PRINCETON UNIVERSITY PRESS PRINCETON AND OXFORD

GEORGE M. FREDRICKSON

RACISM

—

A Short

History

Copyright © 2002 by Princeton University Press

Published by Princeton University Press, 41 William Street,
Princeton, New Jersey 08540

In the United Kingdom: Princeton University Press,
3 Market Place, Woodstock, Oxfordshire OX20 1SY

All Rights Reserved

Library of Congress Cataloging-in-Publication Data

Fredrickson, George M., 1934–
Racism : a short history / George M. Fredrickson.
p. cm.
Includes bibliographical references and index.
ISBN 0-691-00899-X (alk. paper)
1. Racism—History. 2. Race relations—History. I. Title.
HT1507 .F74 2002
305.8'009—dc21   2001055191

British Library Cataloging-in-Publication Data is available

This book has been composed in Dante

Printed on acid-free paper.∞

www.pupress.princeton.edu

Printed in the United States of America

10 9 8 7 6 5 4 3 2 1

For

Donald Fleming,

mentor and

friend

CONTENTS

ACKNOWLEDGMENTS

I n the course of carrying this project to fruition I have
acquired many debts. To Professor Constantin Fasolt of
the University of Chicago I owe the original suggestion
that I write a short book on racism in world historical perspective. Although I did not in the end fulfill his hope that
I would contribute such a volume to a series he edits, I
would not have been emboldened to undertake something
of this breadth without his initial encouragement. I want
to thank the Princeton University Public Lectures Commit-
tee and Professor Nancy Weiss Malkiel, Dean of the Fac-
ulty, for inviting me to give the series of lectures on which
this book is based. Brigitta van Rheinberg of Princeton University Press guided this work from the beginning and
made valuable recommendations concerning structure and
emphasis. Providing very helpful critiques of all or part of
the manuscript at various stages of development were Benjamin Braude, Sean Dobson, John Cell, Norman Naimark,
David Nirenberg, John Torpey, Eric Weitz, Howard Winant, and John Worth. These eminent scholars of course
bear no responsibility for any errors that remain. David
Holland provided invaluable assistance in helping me to
prepare the manuscript for publication.

RACISM

INTRODUCTION

The term "racism" is often used in a loose and unreflective way to describe the hostile or negative feelings of one ethnic group or "people" toward another and the actions resulting from such attitudes. But sometimes the antipathy of one group toward another is expressed and acted upon with a single-mindedness and brutality that go far beyond the group-centered prejudice and snobbery that seem to constitute an almost universal human failing. Hitler invoked racist theories to justify his genocidal treatment of European Jewry, as did white supremacists in the American South to explain why Jim Crow laws were needed to keep whites and blacks separated and unequal.

The climax of the history of racism came in the twentieth century in the rise and fall of what I will call "overtly racist regimes." In the American South, the passage of segregation laws and restrictions on black voting rights reduced African Americans to lower-caste status, despite the constitutional amendments that had made them equal citizens. Extreme racist propaganda, which represented black males as ravening beasts lusting after white women, served to rationalize the practice of lynching. These extralegal executions were increasingly reserved for blacks accused of offenses against the color line, and they became more brutal and sadistic as time went on; by the early twentieth century victims were likely to be tortured to death rather than simply killed. A key feature of the racist regime maintained by state law in the South was a fear of sexual contamination through rape or intermarriage, which led to efforts to prevent the conjugal union of whites with those with any known or discernible African ancestry.

The effort to guarantee "race purity" in the American South anticipated aspects of the official Nazi persecution of Jews in the 1930s. The Nuremberg Laws of 1935 prohibited intermarriage or sexual relations between Jews and gentiles, and the propaganda surrounding the legislation emphasized the sexual threat that predatory Jewish males presented to German womanhood and the purity of German blood. Racist ideology was of course eventually carried to a more extreme point in Nazi Germany than in the American South of the Jim Crow era. Individual blacks had been hanged or burned to death by the lynch mobs to serve as examples to ensure that the mass of southern African Americans would scrupulously respect the color line. But it took Hitler and the Nazis to attempt the extermination of an entire ethnic group on the basis of a racist ideology.

Hitler, it has been said, gave racism a bad name. The moral revulsion of people throughout the world against what the Nazis did, reinforced by scientific studies undermining racist genetics (or eugenics), served to discredit the scientific racism that had been respectable and influential in the United States and Europe before the Second

World War. But explicit racism also came under devastating attack by the new nations resulting from the decolonization of Africa and Asia and their representatives in the United Nations. The civil rights movement in the United States, which succeeded in outlawing legalized racial segregation and discrimination in the 1960s, was a beneficiary of revulsion against the Holocaust as the logical extreme of racism. But it also drew crucial support from the growing sense that national interests were threatened when blacks in the United States were mistreated and abused. In the competition with the Soviet Union for "the hearts and minds" of independent Africans and Asians, Jim Crow and the ideology that sustained it became a national embarrassment with possible strategic consequences.

The one racist regime that survived the Second World War and the Cold War was the South African, which did not in fact come to fruition until the advent of apartheid in 1948. The laws passed banning all marriage and sexual relations between different "population groups" and requiring separate residential areas for people of mixed race ("Coloreds"), as well as for Africans, signified the same obsession with "race purity" that characterized the other racist regimes. However, the climate of world opinion in the wake of the Holocaust induced some apologists for apartheid to avoid straightforward biological racism and to rest their case for "separate development" mainly on cultural rather than physical differences. The extent to which Afrikaner nationalism was inspired by nineteenth-century European cultural nationalism also contributed to this avoidance of a pseudoscientific rationale. No better example can be found of how a "cultural essentialism" based on nationality can do the work of a racism based squarely on skin color or other physical characteristics. The South African government also tried to accommodate itself to the age of decolonization. It offered a dubious independence to the overcrowded "homelands," from which African migrants went forth to work for limited periods in the mines and factories of the nine-tenths of the country reserved for a white minority that constituted less than a sixth of the total population.

The defeat of Nazi Germany, the desegregation of the American South in the 1960s, and the establishment of majority rule in South Africa suggest that regimes based on biological racism or its cultural essentialist equivalent are a thing of the past. But racism does not require the full and explicit support of the state and the law. Nor does it require an ideology centered on the concept of biological inequality. Discrimination by institutions and individuals against those perceived as racially different can long persist and even flourish under the illusion of nonracism, as recent students of Brazilian race relations have discovered.[1] The use of allegedly deep-seated cultural differences as a justification for hostility and discrimination against newcomers from the Third World in several European countries has led to allegations of a new "cultural racism." Similarly, those sympathetic to the plight of poor African Americans and Latinos in the United States have described as "racist" the view of some whites that many denizens of the ghettos and barrios can be written off as incurably infected by cultural pathologies. From the historian's perspective such recent examples of cultural determinism are not in fact unprecedented. They rather represent a reversion to the way that the differences between ethnoracial groups could be made to seem indelible and unbridgeable before the articulation of a scientific or naturalistic conception of race in the eighteenth century.

The aim of this book is to present in a concise fashion the story of racism's rise and decline (although not yet, unfortunately, its fall) from the Middle Ages to the present. To achieve this, I have tried to give racism a more precise definition than mere ethnocentric dislike and distrust of the Other. The word "racism" first came into common usage in the 1930s when a new word was required to describe the theories on which the Nazis based their persecution of the Jews. As is the case with many of the terms historians use, the phenomenon existed before the coinage of the word that we use to describe it. But our understanding of what beliefs and behaviors are to be considered "racist" has been unstable. Somewhere between the view that racism is a peculiar modern idea without much historical precedent and the notion that it is simply a manifestation of the ancient phenomenon of tribalism or xenophobia may lie a working definition that covers more than scientific or biological racism but less than the kind of group prejudice based on culture, religion, or simply a sense of family or kinship.[2]

It is when differences that might otherwise be considered ethnocultural are regarded as innate, indelible, and unchangeable that a racist attitude or ideology can be said to exist. It finds its clearest expression when the kind of ethnic differences that are firmly rooted in language, customs, and kinship are overridden in the name of an imagined collectivity based on pigmentation, as in white supremacy, or on a linguistically based myth of remote descent from a superior race, as in Aryanism. But racism as I conceive it is not merely an attitude or set of beliefs; it also expresses itself in the practices, institutions, and structures that a sense of deep difference justifies or validates. Racism, therefore, is more than theorizing about human differences or thinking badly of a group over which one has no control. It either directly sustains or proposes to establish *a racial order*, a permanent group hierarchy that is believed to reflect the laws of nature or the decrees of God. Racism in this sense is neither a given of human social existence, a universal "consciousness of kind," nor simply a modern theory that biology determines history and culture. Like the modern scientific racism that is one expression of it, it has a historical trajectory and is mainly, if not exclusively, a product of the West. But it originated in at least a prototypical form in the fourteenth and fifteenth centuries rather than in the eighteenth or nineteenth (as is sometimes maintained) and was originally articulated in the idioms of religion more than in those of natural science.

Racism is therefore not merely "xenophobia"—a term invented by the ancient Greeks to describe a reflexive feeling of hostility to the stranger or Other. Xenophobia may be a starting point upon which racism can be constructed, but it is not the thing itself. For an understanding of the emergence of Western racism in the late Middle Ages and early modern period, a clear distinction between racism and religious intolerance is crucial. The religious bigot condemns and persecutes others for what they believe, not for what they intrinsically are. I would not therefore consider the sincere missionary, who may despise the beliefs and habits of the object of his or her ministrations, to be a racist. If a heathen can be redeemed through baptism, or if an ethnic stranger can be assimilated into the tribe or the culture in such a way that his or her origins cease to matter in any significant way, we are in the presence of an attitude that often creates conflict and misery, but not one that should be labeled racist. It might be useful to have another term, such as "culturalism," to describe an inability or unwillingness to tolerate cultural differences, but if assimilation were genuinely on offer, I would withhold the "R" word. Even if a group—for example, Muslims in the Ottoman Empire or Christians in early medieval Europe—is privileged in the eyes of the secular and religious authorities, racism is not operative if members of stigmatized groups can voluntarily change their identities and advance to positions of prominence and prestige within the dominant group. Examples would include the medieval bishops who had converted from Judaism and the Ottoman generals who had been born Christian. (Of course mobility may also be impeded by barriers of "caste" or "estate" that differentiate on a basis other than membership in a collectivity that thinks of itself, or is thought of by others, to constitute a distinctive "people," or "ethnos.")

Admittedly, however, there is a substantial gray area between racism and "culturalism." One has to distinguish among differing conceptions of culture. If we think of culture as historically constructed, fluid, variable in time and space, and adaptable to changing circumstances, it is a concept antithetical to that of race. But culture can be reified and essentialized to the point where it becomes the functional equivalent of race. Peoples or ethnic groups can be

endowed with national souls or *Volksgeister*, which, rather
than being inherited by any observable biological or genetic process, are passed on from generation to generation
by some mysterious or even supernatural means, a kind of
recurring gift from God. The long-standing European belief
that children had the same "blood" as their parents was
more metaphor and myth than empirical science, but it
sanctioned a kind of genealogical determinism that could
turn racial when applied to entire ethnic groups.[3]

Deterministic cultural particularism can do the work
of biological racism quite effectively, as we shall see in more
detail in later discussions of *völkisch* nationalism in Germany and South Africa. Contemporary British sociologists
have identified and analyzed what they call "the new cultural racism." John Solomos and Les Back argue, for example, that race is now "coded as culture," that "the central
feature of these processes is that the qualities of social
groups are fixed, made natural, confined within a pseudo-
biologically defined culturalism." Racism is therefore "a
scavenger ideology, which gains its power from its ability
to pick out and utilize ideas and values from other sets of
ideas and beliefs in specific socio-historical contexts." But
there are also "strong continuities in the articulation of the
images of the 'other,' as well as in the images which are
evident in the ways in which racist movements define the
boundaries of 'race' and 'nation.'"[4] These continuities suggest to me that there is a general history of racism, as well
as a history of particular racisms, but knowledge of specific
contexts is necessary to an understanding of the varying
forms and functions of the generic phenomenon with
which we are concerned.

My theory or conception of racism, therefore, has two components: *difference* and *power*. It originates from a mind-set that regards "them" as different from "us" in ways that are permanent and unbridgeable. This sense of difference provides a motive or rationale for using our power advantage to treat the ethnoracial Other in ways that we would regard as cruel or unjust if applied to members of our own group. The possible consequences of this nexus of attitude and action range from unofficial but pervasive social discrimination at one end of the spectrum to genocide at the other, with government-sanctioned segregation, colonial subjugation, exclusion, forced deportation (or "ethnic cleansing"), and enslavement among the other variations on the theme. In all manifestations of racism from the mildest to the most severe, what is being denied is the possibility that the racializers and the racialized can coexist in the same society, except perhaps on the basis of domination and subordination. Also rejected is any notion that individuals can obliterate ethnoracial difference by changing their identities.

The French sociologist Pierre-André Taguieff has distinguished between two distinctive varieties or "logics" of racism—"le racisme d'exploitation" and "le racisme d'extermination."[5] One might also call the two possibilities the racism of inclusion and the racism of exclusion. Both are racist because the inclusionary variant permits incorporation only on the basis of a rigid hierarchy justified by a belief in permanent, unbridgeable differences between the associated groups, while the exclusionary type goes further and finds no way at all that the groups can coexist in the same society. The former would obviously apply most readily to white supremacy and the latter to antisemitism. But historical reality is too messy to enable us to use these dichotomies consistently in a group-specific way. For long periods in European history, Jews were tolerated so long as they stayed in "their place" (the ghetto), whereas African Americans migrating to the northern states during the era of slavery and afterward often found themselves exposed to what the psychologist Joel Kovel has called "aversive racism" to distinguish it from the "dominative" variety that he finds ascendant in the South.[6] Antebellum "black laws" forbidding the immigration of free African Americans into several Midwestern states were conspicuous examples of aversive racism, as were the various schemes for colonizing blacks outside of the United States. Depending on the circumstances of the dominant group, and what uses, if any, it has for the subalterns, the logic of racism can shift from inclusionary to exclusionary and vice versa.

My conception may at first seem too broad to have the historical specificity that I promised to give it. It is possible that relations among peoples before the late Middle Ages were sometimes characterized by the kind of hostility and exclusiveness that betokens racism. But it was more common, if not universal, to assimilate strangers into the tribe or nation, if they were willing to be so incorporated. There might be non-Western forms of prejudice and ethnocentrism that would be hard to exclude under the terms of my definition. The traditional belief of the Japanese that only people of their own stock can truly understand and appreciate their culture, with the resulting discrimination against Japanese-born Koreans, might be an example.[7] Another might be the feudal-type hegemony exercised by the ethnically distinct Tutsi herdsmen over the Hutu agriculturalists in Rwanda and Burundi before colonization.[8] But I will concentrate on racism in Europe and its colonial extensions since the fifteenth century for several reasons. First, even if it has existed elsewhere in rudimentary form, the virus of racism did not infect Europe itself prior to the period between the late medieval and early modern periods. Hence we can study its emergence in a time and place for which we have a substantial historical record. Second, the varieties of racism that developed in the West had greater impact on world history than any functional equivalent that we might detect in another era or part of the world. Third, the logic of racism was fully worked out, elaborately implemented, and carried to its ultimate extremes in the West, while at the same time being identified, condemned, and resisted from within the same cultural tradition.

What makes Western racism so autonomous and conspicuous in world history has been that it developed in a context that presumed human equality of some kind. First came the doctrine that the Crucifixion offered grace to all willing to receive it and made all Christian believers equal before God. Later came the more revolutionary concept that all "men" are born free and equal and entitled to equal rights in society and government. If a culture holds a premise of spiritual and temporal *inequality*, if a hierarchy exists that is unquestioned even by its lower-ranking members, as in the Indian caste system before the modern era, there is no incentive to deny the full humanity of underlings in order to treat them as impure or unworthy. If equality is the norm in the spiritual or temporal realms (or in both at the same time), and there are groups of people within the

11

society who are so despised or disparaged that the uphold-ers of the norms feel compelled to make them exceptions to the promise or realization of equality, they can be denied the prospect of equal status only if they allegedly possess some extraordinary deficiency that makes them less than fully human. It is uniquely in the West that we find the dialectical interaction between a premise of equality and an intense prejudice toward certain groups that would seem to be a precondition for the full flowering of racism as an ideology or worldview.

Writing an overview of the history of Western racism is possible because of the labors of many historians who have worked on particular aspects of the question. My en-deavor is inevitably an attempt at synthesis, although a por-tion of the scholarship I will be synthesizing is the product of my own original research. Readers interested in placing this work in a fuller scholarly (and autobiographical) con-text might at this point turn to the appendix, which traces the career of the concept of racism in historical discourse since the term (or its near equivalent) was first used in the 1920s. I pay particular attention there to how investigations of antisemitism and white supremacy have, for the most part, gone their separate ways. In the main body of the book I attempt an extensive comparison of the historical development over the past six centuries of these two most prominent expressions of Western racism. (To my knowl-edge no one has previously attempted such a study.) Chap-ter 1 deals with the segue between the religious intolerance of the Middle Ages and the nascent racism of the Age of Discovery and the Renaissance. Particular attention is paid in this chapter to Spain, the first great colonizing nation and a seedbed for Western attitudes toward race. The second chapter concerns the rise of modern racist ideologies, especially white supremacy and antisemitism, in the eighteenth and nineteenth centuries. It concludes with a comparison of the rise—in response to "emancipation" as prospect or reality—of antiblack racism in the United States and racial antisemitism in Germany. The final chapter is mainly an examination in the context of world history of the rise and fall of the "overtly racist regimes" of the twentieth century—the American South in the Jim Crow era, Nazi Germany, and South Africa under apartheid. The epilogue speculates on the probable fate of racism in the new century that is upon us.

Religion and the Invention of Racism

I t is the dominant view among scholars who have studied conceptions of difference in the ancient world that no concept truly equivalent to that of "race" can be detected in the thought of the Greeks, Romans, and early Christians. The Greeks distinguished between the civilized and the barbarous, but these categories do not seem to have been regarded as hereditary. One was civilized if one was fortunate enough to live in a city-state and participate in political life, barbarous if one lived rustically under some form of despotic rule.[1] The Romans had slaves representing all the colors and nationalities found on the frontiers of their empire and citizens of corresponding diversity from among those who were free and proffered their allegiance to the republic or the emperor.[2] After extensive research, the classical scholar Frank Snowden could find no evidence that dark skin color served as the basis of invidious distinctions anywhere in the ancient world. The early Christians, for example, celebrated the conversion of Africans as evidence for their faith in the spiritual equality of all human beings.[3]

It would of course be stretching a point to claim that there was no ethnic prejudice in antiquity. The refusal of dispersed Jews to accept the religious and cultural hegemony of the gentile nations or empires within which they resided sometimes aroused hostility against them. But abandoning their ethnoreligious exceptionalism and worshiping the local divinities (or accepting Christianity once it had been established) was an option open to them that would have eliminated most of the Otherness that made them unpopular. Jews created a special problem for Christians because of the latter's belief that the New Testament superseded the Old, and that the refusal of Jews to recognize Christ as the Messiah was preventing the triumph of the gospel. Anti-Judaism was endemic to Christianity from the beginning, but since the founders of their religion were themselves Jews, it would have been difficult for early Christians to claim that there was something inherently defective about Jewish blood or ancestry. Nonetheless there was an undeniable tendency to consider the Jews who had not converted when Christ was among them as a corporate group that bore a direct responsibility for the Crucifixion. "For the organization of Christianity," writes the French historian Léon Poliakov, "it was essential that the Jews be a criminally guilty people."[4] In Matthew 27:25 Jews who called for the death of Christ cry out after the deed has been done: "His blood be upon us and our Children."

The notion that Jews were collectively and hereditarily responsible for the worst possible human crime—deicide—created a powerful incentive for persecution. If it had been believed that the curse fell on individual Jews in such a way that they could never be absolved of it, racism would be a proper term for the prejudice against them. But the doctrine, as expounded by Saint Augustine and others, that the conversion of the Jews was a Christian duty and essential to the salvation of the world meant that the great hereditary sin was not an indelible and insurmountable source of difference. Anti-Judaism became antisemitism whenever it turned into a consuming hatred that made getting rid of Jews seem preferable to trying to convert them, and antisemitism became racism when the belief took hold that Jews were intrinsically and organically evil rather than merely having false beliefs and wrong dispositions.[5]

In the twelfth and thirteenth centuries the attitudes of European Christians toward Jews became more hostile in ways that laid a foundation for the racism that later developed. Once welcomed as international merchants and traders, Jews were increasingly forced by commercial competition from Christian merchant guilds into the unpopular and putatively sinful occupation of lending money at interest. But in this period of intense religiosity, it was the spiritual threat Jews allegedly represented that inspired most of the violence against them. Massacres of Jews began at the time of the First Crusade in 1096. In a few communities, mobs, stirred up by the rhetoric associated with the campaign to redeem the Holy Land from Muslims, turned on local Jews. Later Crusades stimulated more such pogroms. The church and the civil authorities viewed Muslims as a political and military threat to Christendom, while Jews had seemed to them to be relatively harmless and even somewhat useful. The church valued the presence of dispersed and suffering Jews as witnesses to divine revelation, and rulers sometimes employed them as fiscal agents. Consequently the ruling

powers tried, with varying degrees of conviction and success, to protect Jews from the murderous mobs and roving
bands that perpetrated violence against them in the elev-
enth and twelfth centuries. But even the mobs did not regard Jews as beyond redemption. Most historians affirm
that to be baptized rather than killed was a real option.
That so many Jews chose to die was a testament to the
strength of their own faith and that of their executioners
rather than a prelude to the Holocaust.[6]

Nevertheless, in the heat of killing Jews and pillaging
their communities, some must have questioned the notion
that Jews had souls to be saved, and that they chose to be
the way they were rather than being naturally and irredeemably perverse. By the thirteenth and fourteenth centuries, a folk mythology had taken root that could put Jews
outside the pale of humanity by literally demonizing them.
The first claim that Jews had crucified a Christian child for
ritual purposes was made in England around 1150. Other
such accusations followed in England and elsewhere, often
combined with the assertion that Jews required Christian
blood for their most sacred ceremonies. After the doctrine
of transubstantiation was made an article of faith in 1215
came the most bizarre charge of all. Despite the traditional
notion that the Jews' principal deficiency was their lack of
a belief in the divinity of Christ, some of them were accused
of stealing the consecrated host from Christian churches
and torturing it, thus repeating their original crime of torturing and killing Jesus. (This myth presumed that what
was wrong with Jews was not their unbelief but rather their
evil disposition; like Satan himself they seemingly knew

very well that Christ was the Son of God but nonetheless arrayed themselves against him.)[7]

Increasingly in popular mythology, folklore, and iconography, an association was made between Jews and the Devil or between Jews and witchcraft. In the popular mind of the late Middle Ages, the problem presented by Jews was not so much their unbelief as their malevolent intent against Christians and their willingness to enlist the Powers of Darkness in their conspiracies.[8] The highest authorities in the church for the most part repudiated such fantasies and generally adhered to the principle that the existence of Jews must be tolerated because their ultimate conversion was essential to God's plan for the salvation of the world. But the popular belief that all Jews were in league with the Devil scarcely encouraged a firm conviction that they were fellow human beings. According to Cecil Roth, a pioneer historian of medieval antisemitism, the Jews' "deliberate unbelief" made them seem "less than human" and "capable of any crime imaginable or unimaginable."[9] The verdict of Joshua Trachtenberg, author of the classic study of medieval associations of Jews with the Devil, was similar: "Not being a human being but a demonic, a diabolic beast fighting the forces of truth and salvation with Satan's weapons, was the Jew as medieval Europe saw him."[10] Although more recent historians of medieval antisemitism have found this picture to be exaggerated if taken literally, at least some medieval Christians—a substantial minority, if not an actual majority—undoubtedly felt this way about Jews.[11] The terminology and frame of reference continued to be religious, but the conception of Jews as willing accomplices of Satan

21

meant, at least to the unsophisticated, that they were beyond redemption and should probably be killed or at least expelled from Christendom.[12]

At the time of the Black Death in the mid–fourteenth century, thousands of Jews were massacred in those countries that had not already expelled them, because of a widespread belief that Christians were dying, not because of disease, but because Jews had poisoned the wells. Peculiar to the denigration of the Jews over the centuries, whether as imps of Satan, international financiers, or fomenters of world revolution, has been the role of mass paranoia. Intense irrational fears have been somewhat less central to the racialization of other groups, who were more likely to be viewed with a mixture of contempt and condescension.[13] Jews have again and again served as scapegoats for whatever fears and anxieties were uppermost in the minds of antisemites. Medieval Christians were concerned with the growth of market economies, the enhancement of state power and bureaucracy, and threats to religious orthodoxy from a variety of quarters. Perhaps, as Gavin Langmuir has suggested, some were beginning to doubt their own faith and needed to be reassured by the kind of militancy that hating and persecuting Jews (or heretics) signified.[14] Always a scavenger ideology, racism reared its ugly head in this instance by adopting the garb of Christianity while implicitly repudiating its offer of salvation to all of humanity, including Jews. Medieval antisemitism is sometimes distinguished from its modern manifestations on the grounds that it functioned in a society premised on hierarchy, and that discrimination against Jews was merely part of a general pattern of group inequality. But to the extent that Jews

22

were relegated to pariah status and isolated from the larger society, they became external to the official hierarchy of estates or status groups and therefore became truly Other and expendable. The premise of equality that operated for Christians was that all were equal in the eyes of God, whatever their earthly station. Those medieval Christians who viewed Jews as children of the Devil in effect excluded them from membership in the human race for which Christ had died on the cross. (They also excluded non-Jewish witches and heretics, but not because of their ethnicity.) The scriptural passage most often quoted to associate Jews as a collectivity with Satan was Christ's denunciation of the Jews who rejected him: "You are of your father the devil, and your will is to do your father's desires" (John 8:44 RSV).

The historian Robert Bartlett has argued that the racism or protoracism of the late Middle Ages extended well beyond the Jews. As the core of Catholic Europe expanded, conquering and colonizing the periphery of the continent, attitudes of superiority to indigenous populations anticipated the feelings of dominance and entitlement that would characterize the later expansion of Europeans into Asia, Africa, and the Americas. If the demonization of the Jews established some basis for the racial antisemitism of the modern era, the prejudice and discrimination directed at the Irish on one side of Europe and certain Slavic peoples on the other foreshadowed the dichotomy between civilization and savagery that would characterize imperial expansion beyond the European continent. "On all the newly settled, conquered or converted peripheries," Bartlett writes, "one can find the subjugation of native populations to legal disabilities, the attempt to enforce residential segre-

gation, with natives expelled into the 'Irishtowns' of colonial Ireland, and the attempt to proscribe certain cultural
forms of native society. Ghettoization and racial discrimination marked the later centuries of the Middle Ages."[15] To
support his thesis that this intolerance was not purely cultural or "ethnocentric," Bartlett describes legislation in
parts of eastern Europe in the fourteenth century that
made German descent a requirement for holding office or
belonging to a guild and banned intermarriage between
Germans and Slavs. In Anglo-Irish cities, at about the same
time, guild membership was being denied to those of "Irish
blood or birth," and "there were to be no marriages between those of immigrant and native stock."[16]

What was missing—and why I think such ethnic discrimination should not be labeled racist—was an ideology
or worldview that would persuasively justify such practices.
Bartlett's account suggests that these ethnic exclusions
were usually the self-interested actions of conquering families and lineages and were likely to be condemned by
church authorities as a violation of the principles governing
the rights and privileges of Christian fellowship. Where a
conquered population had not been converted to Christianity, as in the case of the Muslims of Castile in the fifteenth
century, discrimination on religious grounds could be justified. But where the natives had embraced Catholicism, unequal treatment is best regarded as an illicit form of group
nepotism, lacking the full legitimacy that a racial order
would seem to require. The notion that Jews in particular
were malevolent beings in league with the Devil provided
such an ideology and gave antisemitism an intensity and

durability that prejudice against the peripheral Europeans would never quite attain. Suspicions that recent Slavic or Scandinavian converts had not fully internalized the true faith, and might even remain secret pagans, may well have been justified in some cases. But unless—or until—it was presumed that such infidelity was organic and carried in the blood, it would not be proper to describe such an attitude as racist.

It remains true, however, that medieval Europe was a "persecuting society," increasingly intolerant, not only of Jews, but also of lepers and anyone whose beliefs or behavior smacked of heresy or deviance at a time when religious and moral conformity were being demanded more insistently than ever before.[17] It stands to reason that such a drive for uniformity and homogeneity would engender resistance to cultural pluralism and provide fertile soil for ethnic intolerance. Encouraging and exacerbating this heterophobia were the tensions and anxieties resulting from momentous social, economic, and political changes. The gradual consolidation of countries such as England, France, and Spain into relatively large dynastic states with definite borders and a single predominant language was beginning to threaten local autonomy, and an acceleration of urbanization and commercialization were bringing people of diverse culture and appearance into fractious contact and creating conflicts between feudal lords and an emerging bourgeoisie. But in the fourteenth century the incredible catastrophe of the Black Death inspired an especially urgent hunt for scapegoats. As we have seen, the demonization of the Jews in the popular Christian mind was brought to fruition by the widely believed allegation that they had poisoned the wells as part of a diabolical plot to exterminate the followers of Christ.

If racial antisemitism had medieval antecedents in the popular tendency to see Jews as agents of the Devil and thus, for all practical purposes, beyond redemption and outside the circle of potential Christian fellowship, the other principal form of modern racism—the color-coded, white-over-black variety—did not have significant medieval roots and was mainly a product of the modern period. In fact there was a definite tendency toward Negrophilia in parts of northern and western Europe in the late Middle Ages, and the common presumption that dark pigmentation inspired instant revulsion on the part of light-skinned Europeans is, if not completely false, at least highly misleading.

Before the middle of the fifteenth century, Europeans had little or no direct contact with sub-Saharan Africans. Artistic and literary representations of these distant and exotic peoples ranged from the monstrous and horrifying to the saintly and heroic. On the one hand, devils were sometimes pictured as having dark skins and what may appear to be African features, and the executioners of martyrs were often portrayed as black men. The symbolic association of blackness with evil and death and whiteness with goodness and purity unquestionably had some effect in predisposing light-skinned people against those with darker pigmentation.[18] But the significance of this cultural proclivity can be exaggerated. If black *always* had unfavorable connotations, why did many orders of priests and nuns wear black instead of white or some other color?

In conflict with this tendency toward the fear or disparagement of black people was the medieval iconography associated with what the French cultural historian Henri Baudet has called *"le bon Nègre."*[19] Building on scriptural evidence that the first non-Jewish convert to Christianity was an Ethiopian eunuch, exponents of spreading the gospel honored black converts as living evidence of the universality of their faith. There was an unmistakable recognition of Otherness in this tradition; it seemed to say that *even those* who are as alien and different from us as black Africans can be brothers and sisters in Christ.[20] But in the late Middle Ages, in the period between the latter Crusades and the Portuguese encounter with West Africa in the mid–fifteenth century, a favorable, sometimes glorified, image of blacks seems to have become ascendant in the western European mind. At roughly the same time that Jews were being demonized, blacks—or at least some blacks—were being sanctified.

A central element in late medieval Negrophilia was the myth of Prester John, a non-European Christian monarch, first identified with India, then with the Tartars, and ultimately with the actual Christian kingdom of Ethiopia. Prester John's prescribed role was to join Western Christians in the struggle against Islam, which by the time that the association with black Africa was clearly established in the late fourteenth and early fifteenth centuries had come to mean primarily the Turkish expansion into the Mediterranean and southeastern Europe. Hopes for an alliance with Ethiopia and Prester John suffered a setback in 1442 when representatives of the Ethiopian Coptic Church refused to

bow to the authority of the pope at an ecumenical conference in Florence.[21] When the Portuguese actually reached
Ethiopia by sea from the Indian Ocean in the early sixteenth
century, they were unimpressed with what they found, and
the Ethiopians were gradually relegated to the fringes of
the European imagination.

But while it lasted, the cult of Prester John and Ethiopia
was only one of several signs that blacks could be represented in a positive and dignified manner in the late Middle
Ages. Another was the practice that developed of representing one of the Magi in Nativity scenes as black or African.
(Caspar or Gaspar, as he was called, was held by some to
be the ancestor of Prester John.) Equally remarkable was
the cult of the originally white Saint Maurice, who quite
suddenly turned black—at least in the Germanic lands,
where the association of Africa with Christian virtues was
most strongly developed. Other blacks often presented in
saintly or heroic postures were Saint Gregory the Moor and
Parzifal's mulatto half brother Feirefiz.[22]

The representation of the African as Christian saint or
hero was admittedly a relatively superficial cultural phenomenon. It provided no warrant for expecting that Europeans
would be greatly influenced by it when they came into sustained contact with Africans under conditions that encouraged other attitudes. It does, however, weaken the argument
that Europeans were strongly prejudiced against blacks before the beginning of the slave trade and that color-coded
racism preceded enslavement. The one place where one can
perhaps find an anticipation of antiblack racism in the late
Middle Ages is in fourteenth- and early-fifteenth-century
Iberia. Here the association of blackness with slavery was

apparently already being made. According to historian James H. Sweet, it was during the period when Christians and Muslims coexisted in Iberia that the former learned from the latter to identify blackness with servitude.[23]

Historians Bernard Lewis and William McKee Evans have presented much evidence to support the view that the Islamic world preceded the Christian in representing sub-Saharan Africans as descendants of Ham, who were cursed and condemned to perpetual bondage because of their ancestor's mistreatment of his father, Noah, as described in an obscure passage in Genesis.[24] Although medieval Arabs and Moors had white slaves as well as black and thus did not practice the purely racial slavery that Europeans carried to the New World in the sixteenth and seventeenth centuries, they generally assigned blacks the most menial and degrading tasks. In southern Iberia the most conspicuous slaves of light-skinned or tawny Moorish masters were black Africans, and it was natural for Christians, as well as Muslims, to begin to associate sub-Saharan African ancestry with lifetime servitude. When Portuguese navigators acquired slaves of their own as a result of their voyages along the Guinea Coast in the mid- to late fifteenth century and offered them for sale in the port cities of Christian Iberia, the identification of black skins with servile status was complete. Hence even before the discovery of America, some Iberian Christians were more likely to conceive of blacks as destined by God to be "hewers of wood and carriers of water" than to view them as exemplars of the Christian virtues.[25]

The fact that Europeans were ceasing to enslave other Europeans at the time when African slaves became sud-

denly and readily available was at the root of white supremacist attitudes and policies; although, for reasons that remain to be explored, it took a considerable time for
antiblack racism to crystallize into a fully elaborated ideology. Once maritime contacts were established with West
Africa, the acquisition of slaves was relatively easy. Slavery
and trading in slaves were well developed in West Africa
before the arrival of the Portuguese. As John Thornton has
shown, productive and remunerative economic activity in
precolonial Africa depended heavily on slavery. Property in
land was not recognized in custom or law, but the owner-
ship of people's labor was. Slavery in Africa may have been
very different in practice from what developed on the plantations of the New World, but the principle that human
beings could be owned as instruments of production was
well established. Consequently Europeans did not generally
have to capture their own slaves; African rulers and slave
merchants were happy to do it for them.[26]

The practice of holding whites as slaves had been in
gradual decline in Europe since the early Middle Ages,
when the custom of ransoming or exchanging prisoners of
war began to replace the practice of enslavement. Furthermore, it had come to seem wrong to enslave other Christians, although heathens remained fair game. Africans were
not only available for purchase, but they were non-Chris-
tians. Hence the temptation to acquire them and to treat
them as unfree was a powerful one. It could even be rationalized as a missionary project: their souls might be saved
through contact with believers. Initially skin color probably
had relatively little to do with it, except as a means of identification or possibly as an indication of radical Otherness

that made it psychologically easier to treat them with the brutality that the slave trade often necessitated.[27] The conversions of the last pagan Slavs of eastern Europe and Russia meant that there were virtually no European populations available for enslavement under the religious sanction. If there had been, would they have toiled alongside Africans on New World plantations? Quite possibly, but of course it is impossible to prove a counterfactual. What seems clear, however, is that the initial purchase and transport of African slaves by Europeans could easily be justified in terms of religious and legal status without recourse to an explicit racism.

Closer to modern racism, arguably its first real anticipation, was the treatment of Jewish converts to Christianity in fifteenth- and sixteenth-century Spain. *Conversos* were identified and discriminated against because of the belief held by some Christians that the impurity of their blood made them incapable of experiencing a true conversion. In the twelfth and thirteenth centuries, Spain was, by medieval standards, a tolerant plural society in which Christians, Muslims, and Jews coexisted in relative harmony under Christian monarchs who accorded a substantial degree of self-government to each religious community.[28] But in the late fourteenth and early fifteenth centuries an intensification of the conflict with the Moors heightened religious zeal and engendered an increase in discrimination against Muslims and Jews. For Jews the growing intolerance turned violent in 1391, when a wave of pogroms swept through the kingdoms of Castille and Aragon. As in earlier pogroms in northern Europe, Jews were given the choice of conversion or death, but unlike the Jews of the Rhineland at the time of the Black Death in the mid–fourteenth century, a large proportion of the persecuted Spanish Jews chose to convert rather than become martyrs to their faith.[29]

In 1412, discriminatory legislation created another mass of converts. Finally, when Jews as such were expelled from Spain in 1492, many chose baptism as an alternative to expatriation. Consequently Spain's population in the fifteenth and sixteenth centuries included a group unique in Europe composed of hundreds of thousands, possibly about half a million formerly Jewish "New Christians" or *conversos*. The sheer numbers of converts made traditional forms of assimilation more difficult. Rather than absorption of small numbers of individuals or families into Christian society, it was now a question of the incorporation of what amounted to a substantial ethnic group that, despite its change of religious affiliation, retained elements of cultural distinctiveness.[30]

Historians of Jews and Judaism disagree on the extent to which these conversions created believing Christians or secret Jews. There is no doubt, however, that the Inquisition proceeded from the assumption that Jewish ancestry per se justified the suspicion of covert "judaizing." Both doctrinal heresy and enmity toward Christians came to be seen as the likely, even inevitable, consequence of having Jewish "blood."[31] The dominant view of recent historians is that, after the first generation at least, most of those with Jewish ancestry who remained in Spain became believing Catholics. In many cases, intermarriage with Christians diminished the salience of Jewish descent. Yet under the doctrine of *limpieza de sangre* (purity of blood), they could still became victims of a form of discrimination that appears to have been more racial than religious. In 1449, a rebellion in Toledo resulted in violence against the *conversos* who were in the royal service, and their exclusion from public office in the city. In the century that followed, a number of institutions and local governments enacted blood purity laws, and in 1547 the archbishop of Toledo applied this exclusionary principle to all the church bodies under his jurisdiction. Soon certificates of pure blood were required for admission into many ecclesiastical or secular organizations and orders. It is also highly significant that from the very beginning of the settlement of the Americas, only those thought to be of pure Christian ancestry were permitted to join the ranks of the *conquistadores* and missionaries.[32]

To the extent that it was enforced, the Spanish doctrine of purity of blood was undoubtedly racist. It represented the stigmatization of an entire ethnic group on the basis of deficiencies that allegedly could not be eradicated by conversion or assimilation. Inherited social status was nothing new; the concept of "noble blood" had long meant that the offspring of certain families were born with a claim to high status. But when the status of large numbers of people was depressed purely and simply because of their derivation from a denigrated *ethnos*, a line had been crossed that gave "race" a new and more comprehensive significance. According to Léon Poliakov, the French historian of antisemitism, the Spanish attitude toward the *conversos* that developed in the fifteenth and sixteenth centuries implied that "Jews were evil by nature and not only because of their beliefs." Thus, he contends, "sectarian hatred" became "racial hatred."[33] But B. Netanyahu's claim that *limpieza de sangre* anticipated the Nazi attitude toward the Jews overstates

the case. In the first place, the doctrine was applied un-
evenly and enforcement was irregular. Many offices and
opportunities remained open to those with Jewish ancestry.
The nobility itself was never purged of those with New
Christian antecedents. When certificates of pure blood
were required, they could sometimes be purchased, just as
in the Spanish colonies in the Americas, with their system
of *castas* based on color, certificates of whiteness could be
bought by those of Spanish culture but of part-Indian ancestry who could afford to pay the bribe. Nevertheless, until
the nineteenth century it was a definite disadvantage and a
possible cause of discrimination to be of part-Jewish ancestry in Spain. It was a skeleton in the family closet that could
be rattled by one's rivals or enemies.[34]

The fate of the *Moriscos*—those Muslims who were
forced to accept Christianity after the completion of the
Reconquista in 1492—was in some respects worse than that
of the *conversos*. An assault on all aspects of Moorish culture
followed the proscription of the Muslim religion and provoked a rebellion in 1568, which was brutally suppressed.
In 1609–1614, the entire *Morisco* population, numbering
perhaps a third of a million, was driven out of the country,
never to return. But it is more difficult than in the case of
the *conversos* to distinguish between racism and ethnocentrism or "culturalism." More than the Jewish converts and
their descendants, the formerly Muslim new Christians
lived in separate communities and adhered as much as possible to their traditional culture, including their religion.
Ex-Jews tended to be city dwellers, and many belonged to
the middle or professional classes. A substantial proportion
of them retained a pride in their Jewish ancestry and contin-

ued to follow some Jewish customs, like refraining from the eating of pork. An indeterminate number, after going to Mass, secretly worshiped the Jehovah of the Old Testament at home. But it was to their advantage to conform at least outwardly to what was expected of them as Christian converts. The *Moriscos*, on the other hand, were mostly peasants and artisans who lived in their own villages or quarters. Because many of them resisted even the appearance of assimilation, it would be easier to characterize the feeling against them as based more on cultural than on racial difference. But it remains true that *limpieza de sangre* proscribed Moorish as well as Jewish ancestry, and that to be truly Spanish in the sixteenth and seventeenth centuries, one had to claim to be of pure Christian descent.[35]

At the time that Spanish society was being purged of Jews, Moors, and many of their genuinely or nominally converted descendants, Spain was colonizing the New World and encountering another kind of difference. Unlike the Jews and the Moors, adherents to the great religions that challenged Christianity in the Old World, the indigenous inhabitants of the Americas represented either primal innocence or subhumanity. In the great debate that ensued on which was the case, two traditions of thought about difference influenced European—and, more specifically, Spanish—thinking about the Indians of the New World. One was the medieval belief that "monstrous races" or subhuman "wild men" inhabited the fringes of the known world. Some early explorers brought back tales suggesting that the Indians were such creatures.[36] The other relevant tradition or precedent, at least for the Spanish, was the conquest and colonization of the Canary Islands. The native

Canarians, thought now to have been of pre-Islamic North African or Berber stock, were at first regarded as "wild men" and enslaved. But the church protested that reducing such "innocent" pagans to servitude hindered their conversion, and the surviving indigenes were eventually freed, converted, and successfully assimilated through intermarriage into the Spanish settler population.[37]

It is significant that when Columbus recorded his first encounter with Native Americans, he described them as being similar in color to the Canary Islanders. He also manifested the bifurcated image that would characterize European perceptions of Indians for centuries to come. Those Indians who greeted him with apparent friendliness were viewed as simple children of nature who would be receptive to tutelage in civilization and Christianity. But the hostile Indians from islands other than the ones on which Columbus first landed were written off as "cannibals" who must be subdued by force or exterminated. Thus was born the dichotomy of the Indian as either a noble savage who could be civilized or a wild beast who could at best be tamed and at worst should be exterminated.[38]

The great debate between Juan Ginés de Sepúlveda and Bartolomé de Las Casas that took place in Valladolid in 1550 might be viewed as a dispute over which of Columbus's initial impressions was the more accurate and generalizable. The critical question was whether Indians possessed reason, which was taken as the essential indicator of whether they should be accorded full human status. Sepúlveda, applying Aristotle's conception of "natural slavery" to all native Americans, argued in effect that Indians were nonrational beings who could be made useful to the

Spaniards and amenable to Christianity only by the application of force—in other words, by being enslaved. They were, he said in a classic statement of sixteenth-century racism, "barbarous and inhuman peoples abhorring all civil life, customs and virtue."[39] Las Casas, who had personally observed the suffering and high mortality that had resulted from Indian forced labor in the Antilles, contended that Indians possessed reason and a capacity for civil life. They therefore could be converted to Christianity and made useful subjects of the Spanish crown through peaceful persuasion. Las Casas operated on the general principle that "[a]ll the races of the world are men, and the definition of all men, and of each of them, is only one, and that is reason."[40] He did not, however, object to the importation of enslaved Africans to do the work on the plantations and in the mines that was proving so lethal to the Indians.[41]

Las Casas spoke for what became official Spanish policy because his views were in conformity with those of the Catholic Church and the Spanish monarchy. Sepúlveda ignored the crucial distinction between pagans who had never heard the word of Christ, and infidels, like Jews and Muslims, who had been exposed to the gospel and had rejected it. The former, like the Canary Islanders and the American Indians, could be brought to Christ through an appeal to their innate rational faculties. Even if, as was commonly believed in the sixteenth and seventeenth centuries, American Indians were descended from the lost tribes of Israel, they were not burdened with the hereditary guilt of Old World Jews; for they had been "lost" before the coming of Christ and thus had not rejected him or been implicated in the Crucifixion. Only the infidels—Jews and Muslims—

had to be subjugated by force because of the evil in their hearts. But what then was the justification for enslaving Africans who were also pagans rather than infidels? The Spanish authorization of black slavery proceeded primarily from the differing legal status of conquered peoples and those obtained as merchandise from areas outside of Spanish jurisdiction.[42]

More averse to making slaves than to buying them, Spain and subsequent European colonizers either discouraged enslavement of indigenous peoples, as did the Dutch and the French (who saw it as an obstacle to trade as well as an unseemly business), or phased it out in a relatively short time, as did the English in North America. Often permitted, however, were forms of forced labor that did not constitute slavery in the strict sense but came close to it, such as the Spanish system of *encomienda*—the granting to a Spaniard of the right to conscript the labor of an Indian community—and the Dutch misapplication of the legal status of "apprenticeship" to force the Khoikhoi or "Hottentots" of the Cape of Good Hope into pastoral serfdom during the eighteenth century.

If religion rather than race justified African slavery in the beginning, how can we account for the apparent reluctance of Europeans to enslave pagan populations within areas that they were in the process of colonizing? In the first place, as the Spanish case makes especially clear, enslavability depended, at least in theory, on its relationship to the missionary enterprise. The only way to save West African souls, it was argued, was to enslave them, but this was not true of conquered indigenes. However, awareness of the West African's unusually dark pigmentation (even when compared with that of the Khoikhoi of southern Africa, who were usually described as being yellow or tan) soon became part of the equation. Before the discovery of America, it was commonly believed that what struck Europeans as the African's extraordinary color was the direct effect of a tropical or equatorial environment. But when it became clear that the natives of Brazil who lived in a climate similar to that of West Africa had tawny rather than black skins, questions were raised about the origins of African pigmentation. These sometimes led to speculation that the blackness of Africans was permanent, either from some physiological cause or as a result of the biblical Curse of Ham or Canaan. Those Europeans who wondered why blacks, alone of the "innocent" pagans encountered in the course of Europe's expansion, could be held in slavery without qualms (and who were not taken in by missionary rationale) were tempted to see blackness as a curse signifying that Africans were designated by God himself to be a race of slaves.[43]

It is paradoxical to find that Spain and Portugal were in the forefront of European racism or protoracism in their discrimination against converted Jews and Muslims, but that the Iberian colonies manifested a greater acceptance of intermarriage and more fluidity of racial categories and identities than the colonies of other European nations. The failure of Spanish and Portuguese women to emigrate to the New World in substantial numbers was of course a major precondition for the intermixture that took place. Indians were brutally exploited by the possessors of *encomienda* and the proprietors of silver mines and haciendas, but the purity-of-blood doctrine was never systematically applied to those with part-Indian or even African ancestry. An attempt to order society on the basis of *castas* defined in terms of color and ethnicity eventually broke down because the extent and variety of *mestizaje* (interracial marriage and concubinage) created such an abundance of types that the system collapsed into the three basic categories of white, *mestizo*, and Indian. Those categories lacked the rigidity of true racial divisions, because aspirants to higher status who possessed certain cultural and economic qualifications could often transcend them.[44]

Sixteenth- and seventeenth-century Spain is critical to the history of Western racism because its attitudes and practices served as a kind of segue between the religious intolerance of the Middle Ages and the naturalistic racism of the modern era. The idiom remained religious, and what was inherited through the "blood" was a propensity to heresy or unbelief rather than intellectual or emotional inferiority. Innocent "savages" who embraced Spanish civilization and Catholicism did not carry impure blood. Discrimination against Indians persisted after they were baptized, but it was based on culture more than ancestry. *Mestizos* who had adopted Spanish ways could be admitted to religious orders that excluded Jewish *conversos*. The problem that was created for the Spanish by Jews and Moors was that their conversion (especially if forced, as it normally was) did not necessarily induce them to sacrifice their ethnic identity or pride in their ancestry. Such ethnic difference, even if accompanied by a sincere profession of Christian faith, became intolerable in peninsular Spain, if not to the same extent in the colonies, at a time when a strong national identity was being formed. As *Hispanidad* was being constructed in the fifteenth and sixteenth centuries, *limpieza de sangre* was a way of excluding those who did not meet the requirements for a new and more exacting conception of what it meant to be Spanish. The context was the *Reconquista*, a heightened emphasis on Spain as the champion of the True Church, and the growth of an empire that would serve as an arena to demonstrate Spanish heroism and piety.[45]

One might be tempted to draw a parallel with the relation of German national identity to racial antisemitism in the nineteenth and twentieth centuries, but such an analogy should not be pressed too far. One factor that makes the Iberian case different is the role that religion played. National identity and a universalistic religious commitment were made synonymous, and national unfitness was defined as an inherited inability to believe in the One True Faith as defined by the Inquisition. What we have here, therefore, is a quasi-racialized religious nationalism and not a fully racialized secular nationalism of the kind that arose in Germany. (It would take the Enlightenment and reactions against it to make this possible.) The more benevolent official attitude that the Spanish adopted in regard to the Indians was consistent with a belief that Jewish or Muslim infidelity did not taint the blood of the American natives.[46]

Nevertheless, Indians and *Mestizos* were not purely Spanish, and the attitude of Las Casas and the church did not prevent *conquistadores* and colonists from treating them on many occasions as if they were subhuman. Although it was a propagandistic exaggeration, the "black legend" of Spanish cruelty toward the Indians propagated by the English had more than a grain of truth in it. One way to un-

derstand the gap between religious doctrine and social practice is to explore the effect of *limpieza de sangre* on ordinary
Spaniards who could claim pure Christian descent. In Spain
itself, travelers were astounded to find peasants and artisans
claiming to be of noble blood because they had no Jewish
or Moorish ancestry. Sancho Panzo in *Don Quixote* declared
himself to be "of good birth and at least an old Christian."
It was in Spain that a widely shared pride in origin first
became the basis for a kind of *Herrenvolk* egalitarianism.[47]
This *"caballero* complex" was carried to America in slightly
modified form, where it survived into the early nineteenth
century. "In Spain it is a kind of title of nobility not to de-
scend from Jews or Moors," wrote Alexander von Hum-
boldt. "In America, the skin, more or less white, is what
dictates the class that an individual occupies in society. A
white, even if he rides barefoot on horseback, considers himself to be a member of the nobility of the country."[48]

The growth of a religious racism or a racialized religiosity can also be found in sixteenth- and seventeenth-century views of Africans. As was suggested previously, a
purely religious difference could justify slavery. It could not,
however, readily legitimize the retention of blacks in slavery after they had been baptized. The presumption of
"Christian freedom" was of particular importance to Protestants, because membership in a Protestant church created
a sense of religious status that was normally higher and
more demanding than permission to attend Mass in a Catholic parish.[49] In 1618 the Dutch Calvinist Synod of Dort
forbade the sale of Christian slaves and declared that they
"ought to enjoy equal right of liberty with other Christians." But, despite this language, it did not actually require

their manumission.[50] In the slave colonies established by the Dutch and English in the seventeenth century, relatively little mission work was carried out among the slaves because of the masters' expectation that baptism would give them a claim to freedom.

One possible rationale for holding Africans in servitude regardless of their religious status was the myth of the Curse of Ham or Canaan based on a mysterious passage in the book of Genesis. Ham drew the wrath of God because he viewed his father, Noah, in a naked and apparently inebriated state and mocked him. For this transgression, his son Canaan and all Canaan's descendants were condemned to be "servants unto servants." The value of this legend to the ancient Hebrews was that it justified their conquest and subjugation of the Canaanites. But among medieval Arabs importing slaves from East Africa to the Middle East, the emphasis shifted from Canaan to Ham, widely believed to be the ancestor of all Africans, and the physical result of the curse became a blackening of the skin.[51] Medieval Europeans had very confused conceptions of who the accursed really were. Notions of geography before the fifteenth century were so uncertain that a clear sense of distinct continents to which racial types could be assigned was lacking. The curse was variously applied, sometimes to people who would later be considered Asians, like the Tartars or the inhabitants of India. It was also used during the medieval period to explain why some Europeans were the hereditary slaves or serfs of other Europeans.[52] Only in the mid–fifteenth century, with the Portuguese explorations of West Africa, was serious attention drawn to the possibility that the curse explained black slavery. The earliest description of the Portuguese discovery of Guinea referred to a biblical curse but confused Ham with Cain.[53]

The first known invocation of the curse in English writing was in George Best's 1578 account of Martin Frobisher's voyage in search of the Northwest Passage. As Benjamin Braude has revealed, Best felt impelled, as a promoter of far-flung imperialist adventures, to refute climatic or environmental theories of physical differentiation among human beings. He worried about the tendency of such theories to discourage English or European expansion into the torrid or frigid parts of the earth. Would Europeans freeze, turn black, or become antipodal monsters if they wandered too far from home? Not, Best replied, if racial type was immune to the effects of the physical environment—if, in other words, racial identities were fixed for all time by divine decree, as in the understanding of the Curse of Ham that consigned blacks to perpetual slavery.[54]

Between the sixteenth century and the nineteenth, slave traders and those who purchased their merchandise referred frequently, if casually and inconsistently, to the curse as an explanation of why all their slaves happened to be black or African. For many of them, the curse may have helped rationalize holding black Christians in bondage. It undoubtedly helped to inhibit condemnations of black slavery as contrary to Holy Writ. But why was it that baptism did not lift the curse? Jews had also been cursed—for their alleged role in the Crucifixion—but it remained the official view of the Catholic Church that conversion meant the remission of this ancestral sin—although, as we have seen, many ordinary European Catholics believed that the curse had entered the blood. (Spanish bishops condoned discrimination against *conversos*, but only on the assumption that many New Christians were really secret Jews and thus not true converts. They never denied that an authentic Jewish conversion was possible, if unlikely.) To a considerable extent, the irreversible Curse of Ham, like the literal demonization of the Jews, operated on the level of popular belief and mythology rather than as formal ideology. In fact it was refuted by learned authorities, who merely had to note that the curse fell on Canaan specifically and not on his brother Cush, who, according to the standard biblical exegesis of sixteenth and seventeenth centuries, was the actual progenitor of the African race. Justifications of black servitude as a divinely ordained punishment for the descendants of Ham or Canaan were rare or inconspicuous in the treatises and pamphlets concerning slavery that appeared before the nineteenth century. Some proslavery polemicists in the antebellum United States (those who rejected scientific racism on religious grounds) were the first to make sustained and elaborate use of the Hamitic legend to show that racial slavery was divinely sanctioned.[55]

The lack of a serious attack on slavery before the mid–eighteenth century made a fully developed ideological defense unnecessary, but it did not prevent the growth of popular attitudes and beliefs that stigmatized black people as servile and inferior. In late-seventeenth-century Virginia a series of laws made it clear that conversion did not entail freedom. This legislation had the effect of changing the rationale for slavery from heathenism to heathen ancestry and thus served an implicitly racist function similar to that of *limpieza de sangre*. To the extent that Protestants believed, as many did by the mid– to late seventeenth century, that a person of faith should be the slave of no one but God himself, the chattel servitude of a genuine believer could be troubling. To maintain that the state of the soul had no necessary effect on earthly status was an ancient Christian doctrine, but it was losing its force in the face of the Puritan revolution and the rise of radical Protestant sects such as the Quakers and the Anabaptists. In this more egalitarian climate of religious opinion, making a heathen background the legal basis for slavery was another way of asserting innate difference and thus resisting the homogenizing effect of baptism. As in the case of antisemitism a conflation of religion and race in the popular mind would prepare the ground for the more explicit and autonomous racism that would emerge in the eighteenth and nineteenth centuries.[56]

One can therefore trace the origins of the two main forms of modern racism—the color-coded white supremacist variety and the essentialist version of antisemitism—to the late medieval and early modern periods. Since the idiom of this period was primarily religious rather than naturalistic or scientific, it could only be through some special act of God that some peoples could have been consigned to pariah status or slavery. But any such invocation of what might be called supernaturalist racism came into conflict with the main thrust of Christianity—the salvation of the entire human race, which, according to the New Testament, was of "one blood." It was because he argued from this perspective that Las Casas was more persuasive than Sepúlveda. On a popular level the great curses served to make it easier for Christians to treat other human beings as less than human. Europeans might seek to affirm their status and self-worth through the allegation that the blood in their veins was superior to that of people descended from Jews, or because the color of their skin made them the natural masters of Africans. And they could find passages of the Bible that seemed to confirm their prejudices. But to achieve its full potential as an ideology, racism had to be emancipated from Christian universalism. To become the ideological basis of a social order, it also had to be clearly disassociated from traditionalist conceptions of social hierarchy. In a society in which inequality based on birth was the norm for everyone from king down to peasant, ethnic slavery and ghettoization were special cases of a general pattern—very special in some ways—but still not radical exceptions to the hierarchical premise. Paradoxical as it may seem, the rejection of hierarchy as the governing principle of social and political organization, and its replacement by the aspiration for equality *in this world* as well as in the eyes of God, had to occur before racism could come to full flower.

TWO

■

The Rise of Modern Racism(s):
White Supremacy and Antisemitism
in the Eighteenth and
Nineteenth Centuries

When Europeans of the late medieval and early modern periods invoked the will of God to support the view that differences between Christians and Jews or between Europeans and Africans were ineradicable, they were embracing a racist doctrine. The curses on Jews for the killing of Christ and on blacks for the sins of Ham could serve as supernaturalist equivalents of biological determinism for those seeking to deny humanity to a stigmatized group. But the highest religious and temporal authorities generally avoided sanctioning this form of ethnic predestination. Because of their deviation from Christian universalism, these notions lacked the systematic exposition and promulgation that would give them substantial ideological authority. As a set of folk beliefs or popular myths they could create distance enough to dull the sensibilities of slave traders or enflame the passions of mobs bent on killing Jews. But the churches, for the most part, persisted in affirming that Jews and blacks had souls to be saved and were thus the legitimate targets of evangelization. Furthermore, it was not clear that blacks were cursed at all, since the divine malediction in Genesis fell on

Canaan rather than his brother Cush, generally thought to be the ancestor of Africans.

The orthodox Christian belief in the unity of mankind, based on the Bible's account of Adam and Eve as the progenitors of all humans, was a powerful obstacle to the development of a coherent and persuasive ideological racism. During the sixteenth and seventeenth centuries, a few venturous free spirits like Giordano Bruno and Christopher Marlowe included among their heretical speculations the theory that mankind had three ancestors, and that Adam was the forefather of the Jews only. In 1655 the Frenchman Isaac de la Peyrère, a Protestant of Jewish descent, provided the first full exposition of the theory that Adam was not the first man but only the first Jew. The theory of polygenesis, or multiple human origins, challenged the orthodox doctrine of a single creation and "one blood" for all of humanity and could be applied in an extremely racist fashion. If Adam and Eve were to be thought of as simply white rather than specifically Jewish, and if the pre-Adamites were considered black and inferior (somewhere between the descendants of Adam and the beasts of the field created earlier), Africans could be even more effectively dehumanized than through the invocation of the Hamitic curse. Such doctrines might find some oblique support in Scripture (whence, for example, came the people in the Land of Nod among whom Cain found a wife?), but they remained difficult to reconcile with the orthodox reading of the book of Genesis. The theory of polygenesis would thrive only when the power of biblical literalism declined.[1]

The modern concept of races as basic human types classified by physical characteristics (primarily skin color) was not invented until the eighteenth century. The term for "race" in Western European languages did have relevant antecedent meanings associated with animal husbandry and aristocratic lineages. The recognition of superior breeds of horses and dogs obviously foreshadowed the biological ranking of human beings with differing physical traits. Heredity was commonly associated with blood, and titled families were thought to manifest their royal or noble blood through recurring somatic characteristics. In 1611 a Spanish dictionary included among the definitions of *raza* an honorific use—"a caste or quality of authentic horses"—and a pejorative one, as referring to a lineage that included Jewish or Moorish ancestors. The "blood libels" against Jews that began in the Middle Ages were rooted in a belief that blood could convey sacred or magical properties. The notion, implicit in these accusations, that Christian blood differed from Jewish was clearly affirmed in the sixteenth-century Spanish conception of *limpieza de sangre*. But the fact that different varieties of animals of the same species could interbreed, as could all humans, meant that such premodern hereditarianism did not threaten the orthodox belief in the essential unity of humankind. In the seventeenth and eighteenth centuries and beyond, the term "race" or its equivalent was also frequently used to refer to nations or peoples—as in "the English race" or "the French race." Whenever and wherever it was used, however, the term implied that "races" had stable and presumably unchangeable characteristics.[2]

The notion that there was a single pan-European or "white" race was slow to develop and did not crystallize until the eighteenth century. Direct encounters with Africans had of course made Europeans aware of their own light pigmentation, but in other contexts whiteness, as opposed to national and religious affiliations, was not a conscious identity or seen as a source of specific inherited traits. At a time when social inequality based on birth was the general rule among Europeans themselves, color-coded racism had little scope for autonomous development. In the New World, where European pigmentation could be readily compared to that of black slaves or copper-toned Indians, color soon became one—but only one—of several salient identities. In the North American colonies, according to Winthrop Jordan, "the terms *Christian, free, English,* and *white* were for many years employed indiscriminately as metonyms."[3]

By the early seventeenth century you had to be black to be a slave in the American colonies, but it was legal and religious status rather than physical type that actually determined who was in bondage and who was not. In every New World slave society, some proportion of the population of African descent was acknowledged to be free or semifree. In early- to mid-seventeenth-century Virginia, for example, blacks might be slaves, indentured servants, or freemen, depending on the circumstances of their arrival in the colony and, in some cases, on whether or not they were Christians. Blacks frequently sued for their freedom on the grounds that they had been wrongly enslaved.[4] Slaves on plantations might be treated as grossly inferior to their masters, but white indentured servants were not treated much differently, at least on a day-to-day basis. When they bargained for cargoes on the Guinea Coast of Africa, Europeans were forced to treat the indigenous rulers or entrepreneurs with whom they dealt as equals. The black servants who were imported into England and France during the seventeenth and eighteenth centuries were automatically at the bottom of society, but they were not a separate caste below the white lower class. Intermarriage among white and black servants occurred in both countries. In Britain it was more or less taken for granted, but in France it became a matter of official concern and led to restrictions on the bringing of black slaves back from the colonies to serve in French households. (In 1778 the French government enacted a formal ban on intermarriage, but the law was not enforced.)[5]

In the seventeenth and early eighteenth centuries, the status of Jews in Europe improved somewhat (their readmission to England and France was perhaps the strongest indication of this relative tolerance), although religiously based antisemitism remained endemic. The entrepreneurial Jews of central Europe were able to widen their economic opportunities by shifting from moneylending to general commerce. A fortunate few acquired great wealth and influence as "Court Jews"—financial advisers and money-raisers for the Hapsburg emperor and for the lesser rulers and bishops of the German-speaking principalities. "The most conspicuous characteristic of the economic life of Jews in the period," according to David Sorkin, "was . . . the incidence of destitution at one extreme and the accumulation of great wealth at the other."[6] The impoverished greatly outnumbered the wealthy. "Up to the end of the eighteenth century," writes Peter Pulzer, "the great majority of Jews of the German states lived lives that were marginal to the economy and the rest of society, engaged in peddling or begging at a near destitution level. Above them was a smaller middle stratum of small-scale merchants, cattle-dealers, tavern-keepers, rabbis, teachers, and doctors. . . ."[7] Because of the marginal and relatively fixed position of western and central European Jewry, a "Jewish question" had not yet emerged, and outbreaks of virulent and aggressive antisemitism, such as pogroms and accusations of ritual murder, were fairly rare. There was as yet no clear conception of a Jewish race with innate characteristics that made them a despised and eternal Other for non-Jewish Europeans.

The scientific thought of the Enlightenment was a precondition for the growth of a modern racism based on physical typology. In 1735, the great Swedish naturalist Carl Linnaeus included humans as a species within the primate genus and then attempted to divide that species into varieties. This early stab at the scientific classification of human types included some mythical and "monstrous" creatures; but the durable heart of the schema was the differentiation Linnaeus made among Europeans, American Indians, Asians, and Africans. Although he did not explicitly rank them, Linnaeus's descriptions of the races clearly indicated his preferences. Europeans he described as "acute, inventive. . . . *Governed* by laws." Blacks, on the other hand, were "crafty, indolent, negligent. . . . *Governed* by caprice."[8]

The most authoritative classification of the races produced by the Enlightenment was Johann Friedrich Blumenbach's *On the Natural Varieties of Mankind*, published in 1776. Rightly deemed the father of physical anthropology, Blumenbach had no doubt that all humans belonged to a single species and that they had a common remote ancestry. He also recognized that his categories were abstractions or ideal types rather than discrete units. *"Innumerable varieties of mankind run into each other by insensible degrees,"* he wrote. His fivefold division into Caucasians, Mongolians, Ethiopians, Americans, and Malays was a reasonable deduction from what was then known about the dominant physical types on each of the continents or regions of the known world, and his description of each race stressed purely somatic characteristics rather than intellectual or moral traits. He went out of his way to refute the common claim that Africans were "nearer the apes than other men." But as a white European he could not escape ethnocentric bias. He was the first to trace the white race to the Caucasus, and he did so because of the reputed beauty of its inhabitants. He then went on to hypothesize that those he dubbed "Caucasians" were the original human race from which the others had diverged or degenerated. They were, he affirmed, "the most handsome and becoming," having "the most beautiful form of the skull."[9]

Whatever their intentions, Linnaeus, Blumenbach, and other eighteenth-century ethnologists opened the way to a secular or scientific racism by considering human beings part of the animal kingdom rather than viewing them in biblical terms as children of God endowed with spiritual capacities denied to other creatures. Earlier versions of "the great chain of being" extending from God to the most humble of his creations had posited an unbridgeable gap between the human and the nonhuman that was now being closed.[10] The efforts to demote Africans from human to ape or half-ape status that Blumenbach sought to discredit revealed how a purely naturalistic chain of being could be employed to deny full humanity to non-Caucasians. But as Blumenbach's degeneration theory suggested, eighteenth-century ethnological thinkers did not for the most part question the notion that humanity had a common origin and that the variations currently observed must have been environmentally induced. The comte de Buffon, the great-est of Enlightenment naturalists, expressed the prevailing view when he attributed variations in skin color to the ef-fects of climate in the various regions of the world inhab-ited by the distinct races. To Buffon, it seemed obvious that the contrast of black and white pigmentation could be at-tributed mainly to the differing effects of sun and tempera-ture in Africa and Europe.[11]

But an environmental explanation for the variations did not prevent naturalists like Linnaeus or Buffon from rank-ing the races. Buffon, for example, assumed that Europeans were intellectually superior to Africans. He attributed their greater ingenuity to the difficulty of raising food on barren soil. The ease with which Africans could provision them-selves made them "large, plump, and well made but . . . simple and stupid."[12] Characteristics induced by climate and customs were not likely to change unless the environment was radically altered, and no one knew how long it would take for the effect of a new milieu to reverse the "degenera-tion" caused by climate or other physical conditions. Some racial environmentalists in the early American republic fully expected imported Africans to turn white in the more temperate climate to which they were now exposed, but the process seemed to be taking a very long time.[13] There was little doubt among whites on either side of the Atlantic that Africans were currently less "beautiful" than whites, more barbarous in their habits, and probably less intelligent. Hence, for most practical purposes, they were members of an inferior race. The possibility of uplifting them was not foreclosed, but in the meantime there was no reason to think of them as cultural and intellectual equals or as potential compatriots.

The purely aesthetic aspect of eighteenth-century racial attitudes deserves more attention than it has received. In *Outline of the History of Humanity*, published in 1798, the German philosopher Christoph Meiners correlated physical beauty with intelligence in his ranking of human types. "Fair" people were superior in both respects, while the "darker, colored peoples," he deemed both "ugly" and at best "semi-civilized."[14] In his *Notes on Virginia*, Thomas Jefferson reflected the most sophisticated European ethnology of the day when he made blacks the equal of whites in their innate moral sense and gave only a tentative endorsement to the popular belief in their intellectual inferiority. But he had no doubts whatever that they were the uglier race.[15] Both Jefferson and Charles White, a British surgeon who wrote in 1799 on the differences among men and animals, were particularly impressed with the fact that only white women could blush. Furthermore, asked White, "[w]here, except on the bosom of the European woman, [shall we find] two such plump and snowy white hemispheres, tipt with vermilion?"[16]

The neoclassical conceptions of beauty that prevailed in eighteenth-century Europe and America were based primarily on Greek and Roman statuary. The milky whiteness of marble and the facial features and bodily form of the Apollos and Venuses that were coming to light during the seventeenth and eighteenth centuries created a standard from which Africans were bound to deviate. The Dutch sociologist Harry Hoetink has attributed to nations or ethnic groups "somatic norm images" or stereotypes of the beautiful that influence their attitudes toward people they perceive as physically different from themselves.[17] But these images are themselves cultural constructions that change over time. Because of the classical revival, Europeans of the seventeenth, eighteenth, and nineteenth centuries valued extreme paleness, as well as the facial features and physiques thought to have characterized the ancient Greeks and Romans.

While critical to these aesthetic judgments about human types, skin color was not the be-all and end-all. The common admiration for the appearance of North American Indians was based on an appreciation of the physiques of young warriors. Before they became "redskins" in the late eighteenth century, their tawny complexions were either ignored or attributed to artifice rather than nature.[18] On the other hand, the most denigrated of all races encountered by Europeans before the nineteenth century—the Khoikhoi or "Hottentots" of southern Africa—were not black or even dark brown but yellowish tan in pigmentation. They were viewed as the lowest of the low both because their nomadic, nonagricultural way of life was considered highly uncivilized and because in physique and physiognomy they were perceived as deviating more from the European somatic norm than did other (and much darker skinned) Africans.[19] What such reactions reveal is that the predominating belief in the unity of mankind and in the environmental sources of physical divergences among groups of human beings did not preclude an aesthetic revulsion against some non-Europeans as ugly, if not monstrous, in appearance. A heightened emphasis on the physical, as opposed to the inner or hidden sources of human character, was also evident in the greater attention to what was thought to be the "ugliness" of the typical Jew.[20] Aesthetic prejudice may have been more central to the negative assessments of non-Europeans and Jews in the eighteenth century than the tentative and ambiguous verdict of science about their intellectual capacities.

Although the racial typologies of the eighteenth century established a framework for the full-blown biological racism of the nineteenth, much of the ethnological thought of the Enlightenment was without immediate practical application. Before the mid–nineteenth century, as Michael Adas has shown, Europeans did not generally regard their penetration and dominance of other parts of the globe as the result of their innate biological superiority. They saw it rather as the fruit of acquired cultural and technological advantages. In the specific case of British India, he notes that British officials remained convinced that their colonial subjects were capable of being fully civilized long after social discrimination against Indians and half-castes had developed in the late eighteenth century. He concludes from such evidence that "popular racism can arise with little or no validation from the writing of social theorists and other intellectuals."[21]

The obverse of this proposition is also true, as the case of Voltaire illustrates. An intellectual can be a theoretical racist without contributing significantly to the growth of popular prejudice or actual discrimination. By quoting from the scattered references to Jews and blacks in the vast corpus of his writing, one can easily portray Voltaire as the first thoroughgoing modern racist. His direct contacts with blacks were extremely limited, if not nonexistent, but he may have been inclined toward antisemitism by unpleasant experiences with Jewish bankers. His main animus, however, was against Christianity, and he attacked Judaism mainly because of its links to the New Testament and the religion that it inspired. Rejecting the orthodox biblical account of human origins, he contended that the human races were distinct species that had developed separately and with permanently unequal capacities. His opinion of the black or African "species" can only be described as extremely dismissive and derogatory. His reading of the Old Testament and his observations of the contemporary descendants of the ancient Hebrews made him thoroughly unsympathetic, not only to Judaism, but also to Jews. In fact, he anticipated the secularized racial antisemitism of the late nineteenth century by implicitly attributing to Jews a permanent set of undesirable traits. But their defects, in his view, were the opposite of those that nineteenth-century antisemites would ascribe to them. For Voltaire Jews, past or present, symbolized religious fanaticism and intolerance as opposed to reason. (Romantic nationalists would later castigate them for their extreme rationalism.) His disbelief in the promises of the New Testament denied the power of conversion and gave Jews no role whatever in the drama of human redemption or progress.[22]

On another level, however, his general defense of religious toleration and civil liberties promised more to Jews than did the traditional Christian view that they were witnesses to divine revelation and predestined converts. Despite his contempt for blacks, Voltaire was generally critical of slavery and condemned Christianity for having tolerated it. His primary enemy was traditional religious and secular authority, and his ethnological heresies were one small part of a campaign to attack orthodoxy at any point where it seemed to conflict with human reason and experience. Despite his own prejudices, he contributed to the growth of an antislavery based on reason rather than revelation and to ethnic and religious tolerance as a public policy. No thinker better illustrates the dual character of Enlightenment rationalism—its simultaneous challenge to hierarchies based on faith, superstition, and prejudice and the temptation it presented to create new ones allegedly based on reason, science, and history.[23]

The role of ethnology in the debate over the abolition of the British slave trade shows that theories denying the unity of humankind were basically irrelevant to the policy questions concerning slavery and race that arose at the end of the eighteenth century and the beginning of the nineteenth. Edward Long, a militantly proslavery Jamaica planter, attempted to defend the trade on the grounds that blacks belonged to a separate and inferior species naturally endowed with bestial and servile qualities. But most other proponents of the slave trade shunned his arguments. Indeed they provided more ammunition for the opponents of the trade than for its defenders. Abolitionists like William Wilberforce quoted Long's strictures on black humanity in parliamentary speeches to illustrate the callousness, immorality, and religious infidelity that the master-slave relationship engendered.[24]

Until the American, French, and Haitian revolutions, most Jews remained in ghettos and most blacks were on slave plantations, which meant that a "race question" did not emerge with great urgency. Strong incentives to elaborate a systematic racist ideology for the purpose of maintaining domination or inciting persecution did not yet exist. In the English-speaking world, an evangelical revival that reemphasized the spirituality of human beings and their equality under God countered the tendency to deny the humanity of non-Europeans and Jews.[25] The secular Enlightenment, on the other hand, was a double-edged sword. Its naturalism made a color-coded racism seemingly based on science thinkable and thus set the stage for nineteenth-century biological determinism. But at the same time, it established in the minds of some a premise of equality in this world rather than merely in heaven or under God, an assumption that could call into question the justice and rationality of black slavery and Jewish ghettoization. The Enlightenment thus managed to give new salience and potency to the concept of race while at the same time making it possible to question whether its use as a basis for social ranking and privilege was just and reasonable.

The age of democratic revolution that dawned in the last quarter of the eighteenth century brought serious challenges both to the institution of black slavery and to the legalized pariah status of European Jews. The doctrine that "all men are created equal" and endowed with individual rights derived from nature or reason was difficult to reconcile with lifetime servitude and forced ghettoization, unless blacks and Jews were to be considered less than human. In the wake of the struggle for independence from England, the northern states of the new United States of America gradually abolished slavery. A combination of the economic interests involved in the emergence of cotton as a major export crop and the racial anxieties of whites in areas of heavy black concentration prevented the South from following suit and set the stage for the great American sectional conflict of the mid–nineteenth century. The separation of church and state decreed in the United States Constitution, and eventually in those of all the states, meant that the few Jews residing in the early American republic would suffer less than their coreligionists in the mother country and other European nations from the persistence of legal and political disabilities.

The French Revolution seemed at first to go even further than the American in extending democratic rights to previously oppressed racial and ethnic groups. In the early 1790s, slavery was abolished throughout the French colonies. The resistance of planters in Saint Domingue to the decrees of the French National Assembly provoked the slave revolution that gave birth to the world's first independent black republic. At the same time, the Jews of France were emancipated from special taxes, restrictions on movement, and political and social segregation, and they were made citizens of the republic. But Napoleon's rise to power and his subsequent creation of an empire saw the reestablishment of slavery in the remaining French colonies and the passage of new laws discriminating against Jews. Great Britain, which did not have a democratic revolution but did have a potent humanitarian movement, moved decisively against the slave trade in 1807 and became the first European nation to abolish slavery on a permanent basis in 1833.

In their own gradual and consensual fashion, the British also moved during the first half of the nineteenth century to provide legal and political equality for Jews. Britain thus escaped the full brunt of "the Jewish question" that agitated the Continent, especially the German states.[26]

Ethnological discourse in the early to mid–nineteenth century focused more than before on the question of whether human beings were "of one blood," as the New Testament proclaimed, or three to five separately created species with greatly differing aptitudes and capacities. Scientific racism of the explicitly or implicitly polygenetic kind did not take hold in England until after the mid–nineteenth century, mainly because of the strength of evangelical Christianity and its commitment to the belief that all human beings descended from Adam. James Cowles Prichard, the leading British ethnologist of the early nineteenth century, was a staunch proponent of monogenesis, but he nevertheless rejected the climatic theory of racial differentiation that had been so favored during the Enlightenment. He argued instead that changes in the physical and mental characteristics of the races were by-products of a civilizing process that Europeans had undergone, but that most dark-skinned peoples had not.[27] While such a theory might not justify slavery, it was compatible with imperial expansion based on the belief that Europeans were embarked on a "civilizing mission." French ethnology was more open to polygenesis, and the belief that the color-coded races were separate and unequal species of the genus *Homo* gained substantial credibility between 1800 and 1850.[28] On the other side of the Atlantic, an "American School of Ethnology," which came to prominence in the 1840s and 1850s, provoked resistance from the religiously orthodox by presenting reams of "scientific" evidence to support the proposition that the country's three main races—whites, blacks, and American Indians—belonged to separately created and vastly unequal species.[29]

In France ethnological discourse was uninhibited by Protestant evangelicalism and could take a more radical turn than in Britain or even the United States. Polygenesis, or more generally the view that the differences that made the races unequal were of great magnitude and unalterable, had the support of leading French scientists and intellectuals, beginning with Henri de Saint-Simon's justification of Napoleon's reenslavement policy. The revolutionaries had made a mistake, Saint-Simon wrote a year after the rescinding of emancipation, when they "applied the principle of equality to the Negroes." If they had asked men of science, "they would have learned that the Negro in accordance with his formation, is not susceptible under equal conditions of education of being raised to the same level of intelligence as [the] European."[30] A leading French advocate of polygenesis, who later influenced proslavery writers in the United States, was Jean-Joseph Virey, whose "scientific" conclusions about blacks included the assertions that they copulated with apes in Africa and had brains and blood the same color as their skin.[31] Polygenetic theory dominated French anthropology right through the second emancipation of colonial slaves in the 1840s. The proceedings of the Ethnological Society of Paris for 1841–1847 contain extreme racist statements that aroused little dissent. The aesthetic aspect of blacks' inferiority was not forgotten in the increased attention to their intellectual shortcomings. Ac-

cording to Victor Courtet de l'Isle, the races could be mea-
sured through an assessment of how close the faces of each
type approximated the Greek statues of Apollo. There was,
however, something theoretical and unworldly about the
French discussions of black ugliness and stupidity. At times
members of the society advocated, in all seriousness, the
crossbreeding of colonial whites and blacks as a way of improving the latter. Mulattoes, it was asserted, were scarcely
if at all inferior to whites. Nothing could have been more
remote from the phobias that characterized North American attitudes toward the prospect of intermarriage with
people of African ancestry.[32]

The fact that pre-Darwinian scientific racism flowered
in France and the United States more than in England may
derive to some extent, paradoxical as it may seem, from
the revolutionary legacies of nation-states premised on the
equal rights of all citizens. Egalitarian norms required special reasons for exclusion. Simply being a member of the
lower orders would not suffice. Civic nationalist ideology
(operative by virtue of the egalitarian *Code Napoléon* even
when France was having one of its nineteenth-century imperial or monarchical episodes) hindered legal and political
acknowledgment of the hierarchy of classes and orders that
slowed the emergence of mass democracy in Great Britain.
The one exclusionary principle that could be readily accepted by civic nationalists was biological unfitness for full
citizenship. The precedent of excluding women, children,
and the insane from the electorate and denying them equality under the law could be applied to racial groups deemed
by science to be incompetent to exercise the rights and privileges of democratic citizenship. In France, the question

was theoretical because there were no significant racial minorities. But in the United States, a true *"Herrenvolk* democracy" emerged during the Jacksonian period, when the right to vote was extended to all white males and denied to virtually all blacks, including some who had previously voted under a franchise restricted to property holders.[33]

Napoleon's discriminatory laws of 1808 were only a temporary setback for French Jews on the path to equal citizenship. But in the German lands invaded and occupied by Napoleon, the reaction against everything that the French Revolution stood for encouraged an exceptionally hostile attitude toward Jews, not least because one of the egalitarian reforms forced by Napoleon on defeated or compliant German principalities was Jewish emancipation. During the course of the nineteenth century, the Germans, more than any other western Europeans, repudiated the civic nationalist ideal inspired by the Enlightenment and the eighteenth-century revolutions in favor of a concept of national membership based predominantly on ethnic origins rather than human rights. Defining themselves culturally and linguistically rather than in terms of territorially based rights of citizenship originally served as compensation for the failure of the German-speaking peoples to unify politically and become a single nation-state.[34] The civic form of nationalism, in which citizenship is allegedly based on universal human rights rather than ethnic particularities, can become extremely oppressive or exclusionary if some segment of the population is viewed as less than fully human. If, however, biological racism can be refuted or discredited, a polity inspired by the ideals of the Enlightenment could become a racially inclusive democracy. Where nationality is ethnic, and if ethnicity is thought to derive from the blood or the genes, those of the wrong ancestry can never be accepted as sons and daughters of the nation.

The herald of the German reaction against Enlightenment universalism, and the forefather of nineteenth-century romantic nationalism, was the philosopher Johann Gottfried von Herder (1744–1803). Herder was a cultural pluralist who professed respect for all peoples, including Africans, explicitly disavowed biological theories of human variation, and was personally opposed to slavery and colonialism. But his contention that each ethnic group or nation possesses a unique and presumably eternal *Volksgeist* (or folk soul) laid the foundation for a culture-coded form of racism. Although he was in many ways a man of the Enlightenment, Herder substituted a spectrum of incommensurable cultural essences for the dominant eighteenth-century belief in a universal human nature. Those essences were manifested above all in language, but also in folklore, poetry, and the arts. To preserve and nourish its *Volksgeist*, Herder asserted, a people should remain in one place reacting poetically to the same physical environment that had inspired its ancestors. Foreign or cosmopolitan cultural influences were a source of contamination and should be resisted. Hence an uprooted or displaced people was both very unfortunate and a problem for those settled people among whom they were forced to dwell. Herder regarded the Jews of Europe as an Asiatic, desert-dwelling people, clearly out of their element. Showing that he was not a strict hereditarian, he expressed the hope that they could be culturally and politically assimilated, but in the state that he found them at the turn of the nineteenth century, they were "a parasitic growth on the trunk of other peoples."[35]

Herder's tolerant pluralism—his refusal to associate cultural difference with inferiority—was not maintained by the romantic nationalists who came to dominate patriotic discourse in Germany during and after the Napoleonic invasions. For idealist philosophers and writers like Fichte, Schlegel, and their successors, Germany stood for the life of the spirit against the arid rationalism of the French Revolution. It also stood for Christian belief against the infidelity of the *Philosophes*. Initially the French themselves were the main target of the romantic reaction. But the efforts of the Napoleonic invaders to emancipate the Jews of the German states they occupied or influenced implicated Jews in the conspiracy to impose alien, cosmopolitan values on the Germanic peoples. In Germany, "the Jewish question" arose initially when the German "nation" was only a cultural and linguistic community and not yet a unified state. The question of how Jews would fit in when cultural and linguistic identity became the basis of citizenship, and the *Volksgeist* was embodied in a *Volksstaat*, could be answered in only one of two ways. Either Jews had to surrender their Jewishness and become good Germans or there would be no place for them. At the end of the eighteenth century and the beginning of the nineteenth, a liberal assimilationist perspective was ascendant in German thought, but beneath it lurked a deep intolerance of the Jew who remained distinctive. In 1793, the philosopher Johann Gottlieb Fichte, who professed to be advocating that Jews be given "human rights," put the choice before them in starkly brutal terms: "As for giving them [the Jews] civil rights, I see no remedy but that their heads should be cut off in one night and replaced with others not containing a single Jewish idea."[36] Historian Peter Pulzer has incisively described the essence of the Jewish question in nineteenth-century Germany: "Those who governed Germany, and those who strongly influenced public opinion, could not decide between the insistence that Jews should assimilate more and the conviction that they were incapable of ever doing so."[37]

The growth of a firm conviction on the part of some Germans that assimilation was impossible was the mainspring of the antisemitic racism that developed after German unification in 1870. Explicit biological racism was not applied to Jews in Germany until well after it had been invoked to rationalize white American attitudes toward blacks. The older tradition of antisemitism, which stressed cultural differences and, at least in theory, made conversion to Christianity the miraculous cure for Jewishness, survived. For a time an expectation of full Jewish inclusion in German life was reinforced by the liberal conception of the state as guarantor of individual rights, a viewpoint that competed with the more mystical and authoritarian conceptions of the state that eventually triumphed. A transitional figure who embraced the coercive, culturally intolerant, and increasingly pessimistic assimilationism that served as a segue between the old religious intolerance and the new racism was the famous professor and public intellectual Heinrich von Treitschke. When he wrote in 1879 that "the Jews are our misfortune," he was referring mainly to an influx of culturally alien immigrants from Poland rather than to the German-born Jews who he thought still might be turned into good subjects of the Reich.[38]

The closest American analogue to this highly qualified and increasingly tenuous assimilationism might be found in the characteristic attitude of late-nineteenth-century reformers, missionaries, and government officials toward American Indians. The belief that Indians, unlike blacks, were capable of being civilized, but only under conditions that they were likely to resist, gave way around the turn of the century to a conviction that Indian resistance to white ways was genetically programmed and could not be overcome by education and indoctrination.[39]

The United States had its own variant of romantic nationalism in the early to mid–nineteenth century. There was no Jewish question, partly because there were relatively few Jews in the country, but principally because religious toleration and the separation of church and state barred official discrimination on the grounds of faith. The status of blacks as slaves and pariahs highlighted the advantages of a white racial identity but conveyed little sense of America's cultural or ethnic specificity. If the Germans endowed themselves with a "racial" identity and then excluded others from it, Americans tended to racialize others and consider themselves simply human—citizens of the "Universal Yankee Nation" and beneficiaries of what was promised to "all men" by the Declaration of Independence.

But during the 1840s the arrival of vast numbers of Irish immigrants and the war with Mexico under the banner of Manifest Destiny created a desire for finer distinctions. The Irish were at least legally white, and so were the "Spanish" inhabitants of the parts of Mexico coveted and eventually acquired by the United States. In this context, as Reginald Horsman has shown, the belief took hold that Americans loved liberty and showed an aptitude for self-government, not so much because these were universal human traits, as because their Anglo-Saxon ancestors invented democratic institutions in the forests of Germany, carried them to England, and then to the United States. Whether such Anglo-Saxon virtues were inherited in the blood or acquired through upbringing and education was an issue that was left unresolved during the antebellum period. Supporters of the Democratic Party, which appealed to Irish immigrants and kept alive the residue of Anglophobia left behind by two wars with England, preferred to think of a newly emerging "American race," which would be a vigorous hybrid of all the European immigrant nationalities. But these same Democrats were likely to be white supremacists who were horrified at the prospect of any amalgamation of this emerging white American race with any non-European or colored races.[40]

Before the turn of the century, when advocates of restricting immigration from eastern and southern Europe began to promulgate the idea of northern European racial superiority, Americans tried to embrace the democratic universalism of the Enlightenment, while at the same time being proud bearers of a specific ethnoracial identity that was sometimes conceived of as Anglo-Saxon, sometimes as northern European, but most often as simply European or white.[41] The particularistic and universalistic impulses could be reconciled, at least superficially, if it were understood that the capacity for self-government, and the claim to equal political and social rights that went with it, came more naturally to some peoples or "nations" than to others. Germany by contrast came to embrace an ethnoracial particularism that was explicitly anti-Enlightenment and antimodern, one that affirmed traditional divisions of estate or class among the dominant group but left no place for Jews as Jews. Nevertheless, a consistently naturalistic or biological racism was not applied to Jews in Germany until well after it had been invoked to rationalize white American attitudes toward blacks. Surviving until the end of the century and beyond was the older tradition of antisemitism, which stressed cultural differences and, at least in theory, made conversion to Christianity (or at least the renunciation of a Jewish identity) the miraculous cure for pariah status.

Racism is always nationally specific. It invariably becomes enmeshed with searches for national identity and cohesion that vary with the historical experience of each country. It is therefore expedient to narrow the focus to the United States and Germany in the period between the mid–nineteenth century and the early twentieth and attempt a bilateral comparison of the nexus between emancipations—of blacks in one case and Jews in the other—and the crystallization of racist thought and action. To achieve its full development as what Michael Omi and Howard Winant call "a social formation," racism must, in their words, become a "political project" that *creates or reproduces structures of domination based on essentialist categories of race."*[42] The projects that brought racism to ideological fruition and gave it the independent capacity to shape the societies and polities of the United States and Germany in the late nineteenth and early twentieth centuries were organized efforts to reverse or limit the emancipation of blacks in the former country and of Jews in the latter.

"Emancipation" is the central theme of both black and Jewish history in the nineteenth century. There were of course obvious differences between suddenly liberating a people from chattel servitude and the normally gradual and piecemeal elimination of the special taxes, residential restrictions, public stigmatization, and limited communal autonomy that set Jews apart from Christians in Europe before the late eighteenth century. But if we define emancipation inclusively as the process of elevating the civil and political status of an entire ethnic or racial group from legal inferiority to equal citizenship, comparisons can be made. As already suggested, both emancipations gained great impetus from the democratic revolutions of the late eighteenth century. The white or gentile reformers who were active in both crusades—the abolitionists of Britain, the United States, and France, as well as the liberal nationalists who championed Jewish emancipation in various European countries—aimed, at least in theory, at the obliteration of difference through the acculturation and assimilation of the Other. They tended to have a low opinion of the actual cultural and moral condition of those whose freedom they advocated and whose "elevation" they sought. But unlike true racists they attributed these deficiencies to an oppressive environment rather than to nature.

Jewish emancipation from the status of social and political pariahs confined to ghettos took place throughout western and central Europe between the late eighteenth and late nineteenth centuries.[43] The process was relatively painless in England and France, at least until the Dreyfus affair led to a dramatic spasm of antisemitism in France around the turn of the century. But in the German-speaking states and later in the newly unified Germany of Bismarck there was significant opposition to carrying emancipation to the logical outcome of full equality. By the late nineteenth century, political movements to reverse the process had arisen in Germany and Austria.[44] One reason that Germany in particular had a more persistent "Jewish question" was that it had more Jews than its neighbors to the west, but they were still a minuscule minority of the population—about 1 percent in 1900. Although Jews were granted limited rights in some German principalities and cities during the 1820s, it was not until the convening of the all-German Frankfurt Assembly in 1848 that the principle of full Jewish equality was proclaimed. But the Frankfurt Assembly was an abortive, revolutionary effort to unify Germany on a liberal basis. In 1849 the lower house of the Bavarian Parliament passed a bill equalizing the civil status of Jews in the kingdom. But a great popular outcry against Jewish emancipation impelled the upper house to reject the bill in 1850.[45] A second-class citizenship that permitted some official discrimination was the best that most Jews could hope for in most of the states of a still-divided Germany in the 1850s and 1860s. When Germany was unified by Bismarck, full citizenship was granted to Jews, first throughout the North German Federation in 1869 and then in the entire Reich in 1871. But some restrictions based on religion persisted in the member states of the federation: in Prussia, for example, unconverted Jews could not serve the state as military officers, diplomats, bureaucrats, or even schoolteachers. Throughout the Reich, Jews who had not become Christians were often denied access to civil service positions, university professorships, and military commissions.[46]

Despite the barriers, German Jews became increasingly prosperous during the nineteenth century. The opportunities in commerce that opened up in the first half of the century became the launching pad that enabled the next generation to go to the university (admission was not restricted) and achieve success in the "free professions" of law and medicine. Jews also found opportunities in the arts and journalism, while continuing to be prominent in the business world, not only in banking and finance but also in retail trade and light manufacturing. "By 1871," according to David Sorkin, "fully 80% of German Jewry qualified as bourgeois."[47] But the fact that Jews were overrepresented in some lucrative or prestigious fields of endeavor and virtually absent in others provided the raw material for antisemitic agitation. It is in the context of this asymmetrical pattern of exclusion and success that "the Jewish question" was discussed in late-nineteenth-century Germany. Exclusions from governmental and military service reflected the prejudice that continued to exist, primarily or at least nominally on religious grounds. The success in some other areas aroused anxieties about Jewish power and potential domination among people who tended to believe that emancipation had gone too far. Fear of Jewish success became in the minds of pioneer racists like Wilhelm Marr, who coined the term "antisemitism" and founded the Anti-Semitic League, a settled conviction that Jews were well on their way to establishing their hegemony over those of pure German descent. Marr's book *The Victory of the Jews over the Germans*, published in 1879, was the first systematic presentation from a secular perspective of the view that Jews were corrupt by nature and not because of their beliefs.[48] Marr was the earliest of many theorists who argued that Jews were innately evil and beyond redemption. In 1880, Karl Eugen Dühring published *The Jewish Question as a Problem of Racial Character*, a fuller and more sophisticated exposition of the new racist antisemitism.[49] The time would come, Marr, Dühring, and others warned, when the German victims of Jewish aggression would strike back and punish the Jews for their diabolical conspiracies.

In the United States racism as an ideology of inherent black inferiority emerged into the clear light of day in reaction to the rise of northern abolitionism in the 1830s—as a response to the radical demands for emancipation at a time when the federal government was committed to the protection of slavery.[50] Defenders of black servitude needed a justification of the institution that was consistent with the decline of social deference and the extension of suffrage rights among white males, a democratization process that took place in the South as well as the North. They found it in theories that made white domination and black subservience seem natural and unavoidable. Some proslavery politicians and publicists had recourse to the American School of Ethnology and its contention that the "types of mankind" were created separate and unequal. But this apparent revision of the book of Genesis was unpalatable to many of the orthodox evangelical Christians who were becoming increasingly influential in the religious life of the South. Those who were versed in scientific ethnology but wished to avoid contradicting the Genesis story simply adopted the eighteenth-century theory that blacks had degenerated from the original race of white Adamites, and then went on to contend that the deviation had become irreversible. They could thus preserve the concept of inherent black inferiority and slavishness without overtly contradicting Scripture.[51] Popular among less sophisticated religious defenders of slavery was the reassertion of the hoary myth that God had placed a curse on the allegedly black descendants of Ham, condemning them to be "hewers of wood and carriers of water" or "servants unto servants."[52]

It was, however, the hostile and discriminatory treatment of the "free" blacks of the northern and border states, who had been emancipated after the Revolution, that showed American white supremacy in its starkest form. Slavery was a legal status that could be, and often was, defended on grounds other than race. One religious defense was simply that slavery had existed in biblical times, was never condemned by Christ, and therefore could not be regarded as sinful (the standard charge of abolitionists). Conservatives who had refused to adapt to "the age of the common man" declared that a social hierarchy with a menial class at the bottom was essential to any society, although some special reason still had to be found why blacks (and only blacks) were at the base of the pyramid.[53] But the segregation, discrimination, and violence that were visited upon the ex-slaves in areas where slavery had been abolished, or where large-scale manumission had occurred, conveyed the clear message that being the wrong color was an insuperable obstacle—in and of itself—to membership in the nation.[54] When the Supreme Court declared in the Dred Scott decision of 1857 that free blacks could not be citizens of the United States, because the framers of the

Constitution had assumed that they had "no rights which the white man was bound to respect," the racist foundation of the American polity was laid bare.

But the decision was in effect for only about a decade. The slaves' emancipation occurred in 1863 as the by-product of a war to save the Union from southern secession. During the Reconstruction period that followed the war, the exigencies of the struggle between the Congress and President Andrew Johnson over the terms under which the seceded states could be readmitted to the Union led to the nullification of the Dred Scott decision. The Fourteenth Amendment, ratified in 1868, wrote equal citizenship for all people born in the United States (except "Indians not taxed") into the Constitution. But the federal effort to enforce civic and political equality for blacks during Reconstruction failed because the government proved unwilling or unable to commit sufficient resources or apply enough force to overcome the violent white resistance to black equality that erupted in the South. Antiblack racism peaked in the period between the end of Reconstruction and the First World War, the era that historian Rayford W. Logan has called the "nadir" of the African American experience.[55]

Emancipation could not be carried to completion because it exceeded the capacity of white Americans—in the North as well as in the South—to think of blacks as genuine equals. A sectional consensus emerged after Reconstruction to the effect that the nation was well rid of slavery, an institution that had retarded the economic development and prosperity that a system of capitalism based on wage labor now made possible. But efforts to extend the meaning of emancipation to include black civil and political equality awakened the demons of racism to a greater extent than the polemical defense of slavery had done. The rhetoric of the latter had been leavened by a good deal of condescending paternalism that had stressed the inherently "childlike" nature of African Americans. Postwar racism, especially in some of its popular manifestations, portrayed black males as beasts lusting after white women, some of whom needed to be hanged or burned alive by lynch mobs to keep the rest properly cowed and respectful of white authority.[56]

These two flawed or limited late-nineteenth-century emancipations—of the Jews in Germany and of blacks in the United States—may seem very different in both context and character. But there are some intriguing analogues that make a close comparison worthwhile, even if, in the end, the differences are more significant than the similarities. In both cases, first of all, federalism served as an obstacle to equal citizenship. The American Civil War may have determined that a state cannot be sovereign, but resolution of this constitutional issue did not prevent the states from having rights that could, given a Supreme Court respectful of their prerogatives, make it extremely difficult to protect blacks from discrimination. As we have already seen, German citizenship in the Reich after 1871 did not prevent discrimination on the state level under the cover of established religion. Second, in both the United States and Germany, rapid industrialization and economic growth gave rise to situations where members of the majority were in competition or at least potential competition with members of the outgroup for jobs or other economic opportunities—something that would have been inconceivable in the era of the ghetto and the slave plantation.[57]

A third similarity is that in both cases the success of emancipation depended on the fortunes of a liberal-to-radical political movement. It is one of the great commonplaces of modern German history that the fate of the Jews was linked to the fate of liberalism. Emancipation occurred at a time when Bismarck was allied with the center-left National Liberals. When he repudiated the Liberals in 1879 and associated himself with conservative and aristocratic political elements, the situation of the Jews immediately worsened and political antisemitism emerged for the first time.[58] The rights of blacks were similarly dependent on one of the majority political parties or factions—the Radical Republicans—who had passed the Reconstruction Acts of 1867 and 1868, partly out of idealism and partly out of political calculation. (They hoped to use black votes to gain political leverage in the southern states.) Analogous to the way that the decline of liberalism in Germany had made Jews vulnerable to antisemitic assaults, the Republicans' failure to prevent the South from becoming solidly Democratic after 1876, along with a decline of the influence of the Radical element within the national party, exposed blacks to white supremacist terror and Jim Crow segregation. German liberalism and American Radical Republicanism were by no means identical. The former was more elitist and less committed to popular democracy than the latter. But if newly freed African Americans could think of themselves as fully enfranchised citizens of a democratic polity, German Jews had good reason to think of themselves as part of a new elite based on achievement rather than birth. By the early twentieth century, liberalism had lost much of its ideological influence in Germany and Austria, leaving middle-class Jews without powerful political allies. In the United States, the Republicans had become a pro-business party with little further interest in the rights of blacks, while the Democrats appealed to a coalition of southern whites and northern working-class immigrants and were therefore even less friendly to black aspirations.

Concomitant with the loss of political allies was the rise of parties and factions committed to exploiting Negrophobia or antisemitism. White supremacy was the central rallying cry of the post-Reconstruction southern Democrats, to be stressed whenever disadvantaged whites unfurled the banner of class grievance and challenged the elite of planters and businessmen who controlled the party machinery and the state and local governments that served their interests.[59] In Germany, an antisemitic party first had an impact in the election of 1881, but its success was engineered from above by Bismarck and the Conservatives, who were using hostility to the Jews to lure middle-class voters away from the Liberals. In the 1890s a more spontaneous and populist antisemitism entered the electoral arena with enough success to induce the Conservatives to emulate their tactics. The incorporation of an antisemitic appeal into the Conservative program led to the decline and disappearance of the single-issue anti-Jewish parties by the late 1890s. Like the Democrats in the southern United States, the German Conservatives learned that racism could be used, whenever expedient or necessary, to steal the thunder of their populist rivals and keep themselves in firm control.[60]

Although it is more accidental or contingent than the other similarities, both German Jews and American blacks were impeded in their struggles for equality by the international economic downturn that began in 1873. In Germany the crash raised doubts about who benefited from financial capitalism, and drew attention to the Jews who had been involved in some of the failed financial schemes of the day. The notion that Jewish swindlers had fleeced German investors became a staple of antisemitic propaganda from that time on.[61] No one blamed African Americans for the Panic of 1873, but some of the remaining Republican-dominated state governments in the South, with which blacks were associated as supporters and officeholders, had overextended themselves and were forced into insolvency. Northerners seeking reasons to abandon the Radical Republican experiment in biracial democracy were given a stronger justification by evidence pointing to the corruption or fiscal extravagance of the "black and tan" governments.[62] The depression that followed the panic gave rise to violent confrontations between labor and capital in the industrializing North. As a result, fears of class warfare helped to smother what was left of the middle-class humanitarianism inherited from the antislavery movement and expressed in the activities of the freedmen's aid societies during the immediate postwar years.[63]

These similar or analogous developments provided contexts favorable to the rise of racist ideologies. In the United States "racial Darwinism" made a stronger case for innate black inferiority than the older polygenetic theories that had seemed implausible or heretical to many. The theory of evolution provided an explanation of how new species could emerge over a vastly extended period of time and become permanently differentiated in their capacities. It also suggested that human races were in competition, and that inferior breeds would not survive in "the struggle for existence."[64] In both the United States and Germany the eugenics movement, which began in England as a biological approach to class differences, was eventually applied to racial and ethnic groups. The belief that government intervention was required to weed out or neutralize inferior breeding stock could justify a variety of policies, including immigration restriction, prohibition of interracial marriage, the forced sterilization of undesirables, and ultimately the euthanasia of entire categories of people.[65]

Nevertheless, despite all these similarities between the context and character of emergent racism in the United States and Germany toward the end of the nineteenth century and the beginning of the twentieth, the differences are even more significant. In the first place, the economic and social competition set off by emancipation involved different classes or strata of society. The freed slaves in the United States competed mainly with lower- or working-class whites. Employers who wished to undermine the ability of their white workers to organize and bargain from strength frequently used African Americans as strikebreakers. It was in this context that a distinctive white working-class racism took shape on the assumption that only white men were loyal to their fellow workers. Blacks and Chinese immigrants (and at times even swarthy newcomers from southern and eastern Europe who did seem quite white) were deemed genetically incapable of class solidarity and were therefore potential tools of exploitative employers.[66] In the rural South, the many white farmers who were losing land and independence during the long cotton depression of the late nineteenth century clung more desperately than ever to the automatic social status that inhered in their white skins. In the words of W.E.B. Du Bois, "the white group of laborers, while they received a low wage,. were compensated in part by a sort of public and psychological wage. They were given public deference and titles of courtesy because they were white."[67] To acknowledge that working- and lower-class whites felt particularly threatened by blacks is not to exempt the middle and upper classes from racial prejudice. But a greater sense of status and security permitted privileged whites to be more relaxed and paternalistic in their relationship with blacks, whom they encountered mainly as servants or service workers.[68]

In Germany, on the other hand, the zone of actual or potential competition between Jews and gentiles was in the middle or professional classes. The successful beneficiaries of the increase in rights and opportunities that came with the unification and industrialization of Germany were doing quite well by the end of the century in commerce, journalism, medicine, and the law, as well as in the realms where small numbers of Jews had traditionally been able to situate themselves—banking and finance. Hence Jews were, unlike African Americans, in direct competition with members of the ethnic majority's middle class. Jewish-owned department stores, for example, sometimes drove gentile shopkeepers out of business. What was more, Jewish businessmen often employed clerks, white-collar workers, and even servants who belonged to that majority. Almost never in the United States during this period were blacks in a position to exert authority over whites. (The fact that Jewish babies in Germany were sometimes wet-nursed by Christian women, a practice that the Nazis later outlawed, highlights the radical difference in the social status of the two groups. White women nursing black babies was of course inconceivable in the United States.) It was therefore not in the working class but rather in the *Mittelstand*, or lower middle class, that resentment of Jewish advancement was greatest. Traditional stereotypes about Jewish unscrupulousness and clannishness created the impression, particularly among those who were relatively unsuccessful themselves and saw Jews moving ahead of them, that Jewish achievement was undeserved and resulted from a malevolent conspiracy to dominate German life. The historian John Weiss has described the dynamic at work: "Belief in the superiority of German blood enabled men of lesser rank and status to maintain their pride as Jews rose rapidly in commerce and the professions. Sales clerks and bureaucratic menials, semi-skilled and with a weak grasp on the lower rungs of the middle-class ladder of success, clung to racism to confirm a supposed latent superiority. . . ."[69] The working-class movement in Germany, which found political expression in the Social Democratic Party, was relatively immune to anti-semitic racism, far more resistant, it would appear, than the American labor movement of the late nineteenth and early twentieth centuries was to the color-coded variety.

These differing economic and social contexts help to explain why racist ideologues in the two countries also differed in their characteristic obsessions. The traditional stereotypes associated with Jews and blacks were given new applications that served immediate needs or interests. Antisemites in the Wilhelmine Reich did not accuse Jews of incompetence or intellectual inferiority but claimed rather that they were innately incapable of participating in German cultural life and were indomitably hostile to it. A reactionary romantic nationalism—fostered by Wagnerian music dramas set in the pre-Christian Teutonic past, the folktales of the Brothers Grimm, and histories of the Germans that portrayed them as an ancient, brave, and virtuous race—prepared the way for the belief in an eternal *Volksgeist* that could not be acquired through acculturation, especially by Jews, whose innate characteristics were considered the absolute antithesis of those possessed by Germans. Germans were spiritual, Jews materialist; Germans were intuitive and poetic, Jews hyperrational; Germans were honest and honorable, Jews unscrupulous and untrustworthy. *Völkisch* nationalism, more than evolutionary biology, was at the core of the racist antisemitism that emerged in the 1870s and crystallized by the turn of the century.[70] It would take the Nazis to synthesize effectively the kind of scientific racism that had not previously focused on the Jews in particular with the mainstream German antisemitism associated with *völkisch* antimodernism. It was the latter, as articulated by thinkers like Houston Stewart Chamberlain, that did most of the damage prior to the 1920s.[71] It portrayed Jews as the symbols and agents of unwanted changes and thus created a powerful hostility toward them, at least on the part of many who felt overwhelmed, disoriented, or displaced by the extraordinarily rapid transformation of Germany from a loose association of predominantly rural and agricultural principalities into an urban and industrial nation. The process took less than half a century, and it was not made more palatable by the ascendancy of the kind of liberal ideology that, in countries like Great Britain and the United States, heralded such changes as "progress" and supplemented them with democratic reforms. Unable to accept socialism because of its attack on private property and traditional values, but nevertheless alienated or threatened by aspects of capitalist development, many in the *Mittelstand* found irresistible the temptation to blame the Jews for what had gone wrong.

Late-nineteenth- and early-twentieth-century German antisemitism differed most obviously from the American white supremacism of the same period in the contrasting ways that the targets of racist aggression were stereotyped. Germans feared that, under modern competitive conditions, which allegedly reward the clever and unscrupulous, Jews might be their superiors. Discrimination was justified, therefore, as a means of self-preservation.[72] Most white Americans, on the other hand, believed that blacks were innately incompetent in all ways that mattered. The danger that they represented for extreme racists was the disease, violent criminality, and sexual contamination that a large population in the process of degenerating, or "reverting to savagery," could present to their white neighbors.[73]

If the "they" were different in each case, so were the "we." Germans were not simply whites or Caucasians; they were members of a superior branch of the Caucasian race—the Aryans. The political purpose of the Aryan myth (which had arisen from linguistic studies that traced German and other Indo-European languages to ancient Sanskrit) was to distinguish Germans and other northern Europeans from Jews. Since ethnologists generally regarded Semites as a branch of the Caucasian race, mere "whiteness" would not do to designate the master race. In the United States, despite occasional doubts about the full claim to "whiteness" of various southern and eastern European immigrants, "Caucasian" was the designation that mattered in the end and served to distinguish all those of European descent from blacks, Asians, and native Americans.[74]

Although still generally valid, this contrast requires some qualification to take account of recent scholarship on the period between the 1880s and the 1920s. During those years, the ideology that political scientist Rogers M. Smith calls "ascriptive Americanism" presented an especially strong challenge to the competing ideology of Enlightenment universalism. It did so by making exclusionary distinctions among European "races," as well as between Europeans in general and Africans and Asians. Nativists seeking to restrict immigration from eastern and southern Europe stressed an association between a capacity for self-government and Anglo-Saxon, Anglo-American, or Nordic (not simply white or European) ancestry. Hence the United States was not immune from its own variety of ethnic nationalism.[75] But what the right kind of people inherited from their ancestors was the capacity to be liberal or democratic in the manner prescribed by the Enlightenment and the founding fathers. In Germany, *völkisch* nationalism was explicitly promoted as antithetical to liberalism and the heritage of the Enlightenment, and it had relatively weak opposition from those who sought to make the national project a prototype for humanity as a whole or even a large segment of it.

At the turn of the century, American white supremacist ideology was based on an interpretation (or distortion) of the Enlightenment philosophy on which the nation was

founded. Science was expected to determine a group's unfitness for full citizenship before it could be excluded. German antisemitism, on the other hand, was based on a rejection of rationalism, universalism, and the political values
that went with them. The American choice in regard to
blacks was either acknowledgment of their full equality as
human beings or their relegation to lower-caste status. In
logic, if not in the inevitable messiness of social practice,
no other possibilities existed. In 1900, the prevailing opinion
was that science had resolved the issue in favor of black
inferiority. But the issue would be resolved differently half
a century later. In Germany there was no such choice or
dilemma, because antisemitism was relentlessly particularistic. According to the German ideology that would come
to fruition in the Nazi era, it is peoples or *Völker* who have
rights, not individuals. As a unique and superior *Volk*, Germans were entitled to defend themselves by any means necessary against alien blood and values. The crimes against
humanity perpetrated by Germans in the twentieth century were rationalized as much by the idealization of themselves as by hatred of the Other.

What do these differences tell us about the deep under-
lying factors determining what British sociologist John Rex
calls "race relations situations"?[76] A critical variable in both
of our cases is the economic role the victims of racism
played and with which they had become identified. Jews in
Germany and central Europe were perceived as "an entrepreneurial minority," the kind of group that is likely to be
deeply resented and readily turned into a scapegoat when
conditions are unstable and times are hard. Total elimination of the group by deportation or worse is likely to be

proposed by its domestic enemies and is sometimes acted upon. Other examples of such minorities would be the Indians of East Africa and the Chinese of Southeast Asia.[77] African Americans, on the other hand, spent most of their first three hundred years on the North American continent as a servile labor force. Slave masters or landlords with sharecroppers have a stake in the preservation of the subordinated group because its labor is essential to their prosperity. So long as members of the group stay "in their place," they may be treated with the paternalism that is often associated with vast power differentials. But if they seek to rise out of their place and demand equal rights with members of the dominant group, they are likely to be exposed to a furious and violent form of racist reprisal.[78]

But the stereotypes that economic relationships have produced or reinforced may survive a change in the actual economic functions performed by the groups. Some Jews originally became members of an entrepreneurial minority because of medieval religious prejudices, and the occupational diversification that followed their emancipation in the nineteenth century did not eradicate the image of them as usurious moneylenders and devious traders. The migration of blacks in the United States from the directly oppressive conditions in southern rural areas to the somewhat freer atmosphere of the urban North did not alter the conviction of most whites that they were lower-caste people, born to serve. A culture of racism, once established, can be adapted to more than one agenda and is difficult to eradicate.

The political context is another variable that has independent significance. As we have seen, the American conception of citizenship had to include blacks once their full humanity was acknowledged. But the logical outcome of the blood-based folk nationalism increasingly embraced by the Germans was the total exclusion or elimination of Jews. The implications of this difference would become apparent only in the mid–twentieth century. If we take 1900 as our vantage point, there is no question that the American color line was much more rigid than the barriers between Jews and gentiles in Germany. Perhaps future developments in Germany were not inevitable. Without further crises, frustrations, and ideological developments, Jewish assimilation into a more tolerant and pluralist Germany might well have occurred. Similarly, Americans might not have repudiated their legalized racial caste system and embraced public equality in the 1960s if it had not been for some domestic and international political contingencies. Historical preconditions do not usually become determinants unless there are some intervening circumstances or contingencies.[79]

Perhaps the most profound lesson to be drawn from the comparison concerns the relation of racism to modernity or modernization. Sources of resistance to capitalist economic development and the individualistic values that went with it were significantly weaker in the United States than in Europe, and perhaps stronger in Germany than in any other western European nation.[80] Jewish immigrants, in the long run at least, adapted well to the American modernist ethos and prospered within it. Blacks, on the other hand, were associated in the white mind with the primitive, the backward, or the irredeemably premodern. The heritage of slavery and beliefs about the savagery of Africa engendered a white supremacist myth that blacks were an inherently unprogressive race, incapable of joining the modern world as efficient and productive people. If the relative weakness of antimodernism in the United States promoted the toleration of Jews, it had the effect of exacerbating the disdain for blacks. The relation of the two groups to America's commitment to the modern seems to me a better explanation for the relative weakness of American antisemitism than the conventional theory that Jews were not needed as universal scapegoats because blacks already performed that function.

In Germany, where modernization was uneven, disruptive, and sharply contested, it was the traditionalist or reactionary resistance to aspects of capitalist-inspired economic and social development and, above all, to the political liberalism with which it was associated in other nations that led to Jews' being made the symbols and putative agents of frightening or unwanted change. If African Americans were not modern enough, German Jews were too modern. The penalties that had to be paid for serving as the antitheses of prevailing conceptions of national character were exceedingly high in both cases.

THREE

Climax and Retreat:
Racism in the Twentieth Century

T o conceive of racism as a natural and virtually inevitable human response to encounters with strangers or aliens is to take the subject outside of history
and into the realm of psychology or sociobiology. But if we
continue to think of it as a historical construction associated
with the rise of modernity and with specific national or
international contexts, we have to conclude that it came to
a hideous fruition in the century that has just ended. Its two
most persistent and malignant manifestations—the color-
coded or white supremacist variety and antisemitism in its
naturalistic or secular form—both reached their logical extremes. White supremacy attained its fullest ideological
and institutional development in the southern United States
between the 1890s and the 1950s, and in South Africa between the 1910s and the 1980s, but especially after 1948.
Antisemitism of course reached its horrendous climax in
Nazi Germany between 1933 and 1945. Several historians
have made comparisons between the two versions of legalized white supremacy, but none to my knowledge has attempted in any systematic way to compare either or both
with what the Nazis did to the Jews. All of these racist

regimes have been overthrown, and the ideologies on which they were based have apparently been discredited. But a final issue that will have to be confronted in the epilogue is whether their demise also means that the virus of racism has been exterminated or that it has merely mutated into new and still-virulent forms.

As we have seen, something that can be legitimately described as racism existed well before the twentieth or even the late nineteenth century. Prejudice and discrimination, fortified by ideologies claiming that the differences between human groups of apparently divergent ancestry are immutable and have implications for social inclusion or ranking, have a history that goes back to the late Middle Ages. But racist principles were not fully codified into laws effectively enforced by the state or made a central concern of public policy until the emergence of what I will call "overtly racist regimes" during the past century.[1] John Cell's conception of American and South African segregation as the "highest stage of white supremacy" draws attention to the relation between modernization and legalized racism.[2] When the unequal treatment of people based on their race is bureaucratized and "rationalized" in the Weberian sense, one can say that racism has been modernized. The most deadly outcome of a racist regime—the Holocaust—required more than antisemitic ideology and sentiment. It was thoroughly dependent, as Zygmunt Bauman has emphasized, on modern bureaucratic methods and advanced technology.[3]

What are the distinguishing features of an overtly racist regime that would distinguish it from the general run of ethnically pluralistic societies in which racial prejudice contributes significantly to social stratification? First, there is an official ideology that is explicitly racist. Those in authority proclaim insistently that the differences between the dominant group and the one that is being subordinated or eliminated are permanent and unbridgeable. Dissent from this ideology is dangerous and is likely to bring legal or extralegal reprisals, for racial egalitarianism is heresy in an overtly racist regime. Second, this sense of radical difference and alienation is most clearly and dramatically expressed in laws forbidding interracial marriage. The ideal is "race purity," and the bans on miscegenation reflect the maintenance or creation of a caste system based on the presumed racial differences. Third, social segregation is mandated by law and not merely the product of custom or private acts of discrimination that are tolerated by the state. The object is to bar all forms of contact that might imply equality between the segregators and the segregated. Fourth, to the extent that the polity is formally democratic, outgroup members are excluded from holding public office or even exercising the franchise. Fifth, the access that they have to resources and economic opportunities is so limited that most of those in the stigmatized category are either kept in poverty or deliberately impoverished. This ideal type of an "overtly racist regime" applies quite well to the American South in the heyday of Jim Crow, to South Africa under apartheid, and to Nazi Germany. Nowhere else were the political and legal potentialities of racism so fully realized.

Many other societies have had a significant racist dimension, and some could be accurately described as "racialized societies," but they would nevertheless fall short of meeting the criteria for an overtly racist regime. Whites occupied a highly advantaged position at the expense of indigenous populations in all of the European colonies in Africa, Asia, and the Pacific. But effective domination and a modicum of respect for the professed ideal of a "civilizing mission" normally required exceptions to the color line for native elites that had either assimilated the culture of the colonizing power (as in French and Portuguese possessions) or were allowed to maintain a measure of their precolonial authority under the systems of indirect rule favored especially by the British.[4] It appears that the only early-twentieth-century imperial power that officially banned intermarriage between colonists and nonwhites, including those of mixed blood, was Germany (a fact that will prove relevant to our subsequent discussion of the origins of Nazi racism).

Latin American societies with significant black or Indian populations discriminated informally against those who were not white or European (i.e., *branco, blanco,* or *ladino*), but did not pass Jim Crow laws or ban intermarriages, which occurred with relative frequency. In such societies, ideologies sanctioning or even glorifying race mixture could in fact serve as an apparently nonracist facade for the persistence of great social and economic disparities that correlated roughly with differences in phenotype.[5] Despite all the de facto discrimination and negative stereotyping that prevailed in the northern United States between Reconstruction and the 1950s, it did not have an overtly racist regime. Many states tolerated intermarriage, and public facilities remained, insofar as the law was concerned, unsegregated. The historian George Reid Andrews contrasted the unofficial racism of the American North and Brazil with the "crudeness and visibility" of white supremacy in the southern United States and South Africa, concluding that "the absence of state-mandated segregation has made racial injustice significantly more difficult to struggle against."[6] But he might have added that the burdens it imposed on its victims were also less onerous.

Finally, antisemitism was endemic to most central and eastern European nations in the early twentieth century— Austria and Poland are the most conspicuous examples— but it did not lead to anything comparable to the massive assault on Jewish rights that took place in Germany in the 1930s, at least not until *Anschluss* or conquest put these nations under direct Nazi rule. Austria did manage to outdo Germany in the strength and vitality of the political antisemitism that emerged around the turn of the century, and Vienna is where Adolph Hitler formed his attitude toward Jews. But racial antisemitism did not gain clear ascendancy over the older, Catholic tradition of viewing Jews as unbelievers redeemable through conversion.[7] The closest approximation to a full-blown racist regime among pre-Nazi European states was Czarist Russia, which anticipated aspects of South African apartheid by attempting to confine Jews to particular geographical areas. But its massive mistreatment of Jews drew more on religious and cultural chauvinism than on an overtly racist ideology. Before the early twentieth century the principle that a Jewish convert "became a Christian like any other" was official doctrine.[8]

A justification for focusing on the admittedly exceptional and extreme cases of Nazi Germany, apartheid South Africa, and the Jim Crow South is that they taught the world a lesson about the consequences of rampant and unchecked racism that eventually changed the standards for internationally acceptable conduct. The emergence of racism as a central human rights issue during the course of the century resulted mainly from the attention paid to these regimes by people beyond their borders. Their rise and fall were major events, not only in the history of these countries themselves, but also in the history of the world. They should not therefore be considered or compared in isolation but only in the international contexts that first influenced their emergence and then contributed to their demise. The story of racism in the twentieth century is one story with several subplots rather than merely a collection of tales that share a common theme.

As has been suggested, modernization or "becoming modern" was a precondition for the overtly racist regimes. Traditional face-to-face hierarchies of an informal or "paternalist" sort, such as those that were found in black-white relations in the rural South and South Africa of the premodern era, could not be sustained in the urban and industrial environments of the twentieth century. The maintenance of white supremacy now required rules and regulations to prevent blacks from taking advantage of the absence of personalized surveillance and thereby getting "out of their place."[9] Similarly, the premodern European pattern of communal separation between Jews and gentiles, with contacts limited primarily to economic transactions, did not suffice to maintain an ethnic status order based on religion and ancestry in a age of heavy industry, big cities, increased social and economic mobility, and the consolidation of nation-states. The norm of common citizenship and equal rights in modern nation-states could turn strong prejudices into systematic exclusions of a kind that could be justified only if the excluded were regarded as less than fully human or, at best, as inherently immature and thus incapable of assuming the responsibilities of adulthood.

But since most modern or modernizing societies did not develop overtly racist regimes, we are left with the question of why the American South, South Africa, and Germany did so. Ethnoracial demography is part of the answer, but only a part. Relatively homogeneous societies without a long history of ethnic hierarchy and division would of course be relatively unlikely to develop racist regimes. (The desire to remain ethnically or phenotypically homogeneous, as reflected in immigration restrictions or exclusions, could involve racist beliefs, as was the case, for example, in the "White Australia" policy. But to the extent that unwelcome aliens were effectively kept out, domestic applications of these beliefs were not required.) Sheer numbers alone did not produce explicit racism. Brazil has always had a larger proportion of people of African descent than has the United States (or even its southern region), and Poland and Hungary in the 1930s had a much larger percentage of Jews in their population than did Germany. Yet it was Germany and a section of the United States that generated overtly racist regimes. In South Africa, where Europeans were a minority, numbers played a greater role, but whites of relatively pure Spanish descent, as opposed to *mestizos* and Indians, have long maintained their position as a dominant minority in Mexico and Peru without resorting to official racism to do so. The persistent strength of the prejudices and stereotypes deriving from earlier relationships—the fruits of centuries of slavery, frontier conflict, intense religious bigotry, or bitter commercial rivalries—would have to be a significant part of the explanation. Negative feeling about blacks or Jews in the preindustrial era were undoubtedly stronger and more salient in the countries or regions that constructed overtly racist regimes than in those that did not.

Another common factor of varying significance in the three cases was the extent to which the racial Other came to be identified with national defeat and humiliation. African Americans, most of them newly freed slaves, gave an essential boost to the northern cause in the Civil War when more than 200,000 of them enlisted in the armed forces of the Union. They were thus complicit in thwarting southern hopes for independent nationhood. Adding insult to injury in the minds of ex-Confederates was the way black votes sustained the rule of Radical Republicans during Reconstruction. After 1918, as we shall see, Adolph Hitler and other German antisemites blamed defeat in the First World War on the machinations of international Jewry and the alleged disloyalty of German Jews. In the South African War of 1899–1902, Africans generally supported the British side against the Afrikaner republicans and were thereafter seen as inveterate enemies of Afrikaner self-determination.[10] In all these cases, the actual perpetrators of defeat and humiliation—the American North, the Allies in World War I, and Great Britain—were too powerful to be within the reach of reprisal, at least in the short run. Scapegoating the available and vulnerable Other was one way of dealing with the bitterness and frustration resulting from the failure of nationalist projects. The impulse to adjust preexisting systems of racial hierarchy to modern circumstances would have existed in any case, but the association of racism with nationalistic *ressentiment* gave to the effort an emotional edge that made extreme measures more likely.

The fact that international wars had a decisive effect on the development of radical antisemitism in Germany and white supremacism in South Africa reveals how the course of world history in the twentieth century could bring race to the forefront of consciousness and encourage the construction of regimes that were officially and unequivocally racist. One cannot fully explain the emergence of these regimes by isolating the "independent variables" that distinguish them from "racialized societies." To be genuinely historical, one must also take into account the concrete and sometimes contingent ways in which the geopolitical history of the twentieth century impinged upon race relations in the United States, Germany, and South Africa.

The Western imperialism that began in the late fifteenth century climaxed in late nineteenth with "the scramble for Africa" and the seizure of new possessions or territorial concessions in East Asia and the Pacific. The ideology justifying the acquisition of new colonial territories by France, Britain, Germany, and ultimately the United States was transparently racist. Rudyard Kipling summed up this ideology in the poem "The White Man's Burden," which he wrote in 1899, in the wake of the Spanish-American War, to encourage the victorious Americans to establish colonial rule over the Philippines. The duty of the superior race, according to Kipling, was to take responsibility for "new-caught, sullen peoples, half-devil and half-child." His trope artfully combined a Darwinian emphasis on the competitive fitness of the white man with the suggestion of a pseudopaternalistic mission to uplift or improve the natives who were coming under European or American hegemony.[11] Racial Darwinism meant, according to Paul Gordon Lauren, that "nations and races progressed only through fierce competition" and therefore "had no choice but to participate in the struggle for the survival of the fittest."[12] The climax of imperialism was driven as much, if not more, by the status rivalry between Western nations as by a desire for specific territories and the natural or human resources that they contained. But the belief in the superiority of "civilized" whites over "barbarous" or "savage" peoples was an essential rationale.

We would be wise, however, to heed the warning of Michael Adas against making racism the ideological essence of imperialism.[13] Although some proponents of imperialism believed that the colonized were subhuman and therefore incapable of improvement beyond a kind of taming or domestication, others affirmed their capacity to be educated and civilized, although the process might take a long time. The view of colonial rule as a lengthy and problematic apprenticeship for civilized modernity can be viewed as functionally racist to the degree that it justified denying civil and political rights to indigenous populations for the foreseeable future. But insofar as those relatively few individuals who assimilated Western civilization could actually gain such rights, the racist aspect was attenuated. Colonial policies that allowed for a kind of emancipation through assimilation, as the French in particular tended to do, were highly ethnocentric, but not, strictly speaking, racist. It was also the case that extreme racists could be anti-imperialists on the grounds that little or no good could come out of close contact with the inferior breeds inhabiting Africa and Asia, or from the effort to settle tropical environments for which Caucasians were naturally ill adapted. The principal English and French advocates of biological racism in the mid–nineteenth century—Robert Knox and Arthur de Gobineau—were both highly skeptical about the virtues of overseas imperialism. When the United States became an imperial power after the War with Spain at the end of the nineteenth century, many of the most fervent advocates of Jim Crow in the South opposed acquisition of the Philippines on the grounds that the nation had its hands full with the problems created by inferior and degenerating races at home.[14] In *Mein Kampf,* Adolph Hitler was retrospectively critical of Germany's joining in the scramble for overseas colonies in the period before World War I. Germany should have let the British do what it could with the colored races of the world, he averred, while Germany expanded directly eastward. The only desirable colonies were those that "seem in large part suitable for settlement by Europeans." Tropical regions that were thickly settled by non-Europeans he deemed useless, and he thought that Germans should have as little to do with them as possible.[15]

Nevertheless, the ideology of imperialism did inspire the architects of segregation in the United States and South Africa. At the beginning of the twentieth century, what became South Africa was composed of two British colonies and two Afrikaner republics (which were then in the process of losing their independence and being absorbed into the empire). From the end of the South African War in 1902 to the emergence of an autonomous, white-dominated Union of South Africa in 1910, the British imperialists who were in control laid the foundations for the policy that quickly became known as "native segregation." Initially the maintenance of a territorial separation between indigenous and settler populations could be presented as more beneficial to the former than to the latter. Settlers, both Afrikaners in the former Boer republics and the English colonists in Natal, were opposed to establishing large "native reserves," because they feared that this would interfere with their access to black labor. For the imperialists, territorial segregation represented a humane and socially stabilizing alternative to direct domination, or what Afrikaners called *baaskap* (literally, mastership). By ceding full control of "native policy" to a white settler minority in 1910, however, the British imperial authorities sacrificed the interest of Africans and made it inevitable that segregation would mean separate and *unequal*—a facade for increasingly severe forms of domination and exploitation. In this case, one can see an imperialist form of race domination evolving into an overtly racist regime, a process that would not be complete until the implementation of apartheid after 1948.[16]

The relationship of Jim Crow segregation in the American South to the highest stage of Western imperialism was less direct but nevertheless significant. As C. Vann Woodward first pointed out, America's embrace of "the white man's burden" in the Philippines and elsewhere around the turn of the century helped to disarm what remained of northern resistance to southern treatment of blacks as racial inferiors.[17] In the South, however, blacks were the victims of such hate-filled brutality in the early years of the twentieth century that even a visiting South African segregationist could find it appalling.[18] In the era of what Joel Williamson has called "radical racism," white southerners did things to African Americans that few, if any, imperial powers would have allowed their white settlers to do to "the natives" once they were subjugated. Not only were Jim Crow laws passed governing even the most trivial forms of social contact, but also black males were deprived of the suffrage rights that many of them had once possessed, and an epidemic of sadistic lynching parties and one-sided "race riots" swept the South.[19]

Relatively liberal or progressive white supremacists—those who believed that blacks were improving rather than retrogressing and could make a contribution to the modernization of the South—were troubled by the violence and disorder. After the horrendous Atlanta riot of 1906, they used their influence on behalf of a racial separation that might provide blacks some opportunity to "develop along their own lines." Black education, while remaining vastly inferior to that provided for whites, survived a demagogic threat to its very existence. By the time of the First World War, the dominant discourse about blacks in the white South was shifting from one expressing utter contempt and even genocidal hatred to one characterized more often by paternalism and condescending benevolence. By this time, of course, blacks had been removed from the electorate, and the Jim Crow system was not only fully established but relatively immune to challenge from outside the South. Hence an analogy with the imperialism of guardianship and the "white man's burden" became more plausible, especially at a time when the nation had acquired colonies of its own.[20] America's mode of white supremacy, unlike South Africa's, originated primarily in the slave trade with Africa rather than in the colonization of that continent. But it gained legitimacy from being arguably consistent with the relationships between black and white that were being forged in Africa during the high point of Western imperial penetration and domination.

Germany's belated overseas imperialism differed from that of England, France, or even the United States in the blatancy of the racism expressed by German soldiers and settlers toward the people they were subjugating. Among the European colonies in Africa in the early twentieth century, only the German dependencies banned intermarriage between whites and nonwhites, including Christian "half-castes." In 1905 such marriages were banned in South-West Africa, and two years later both spouses in the unions that had been sanctified and considered legal before 1905 were deprived of civil and political rights. In the same colony, the Germans also committed genocide against the rebellious Herero tribe, reducing its numbers from 60,000–80,000 in 1904 to 16,000 in 1905. The survivors had escaped what was meant to be a total annihilation by fleeing from German territory. According to the general who gave the order, "The Negro is not bound by any treaty but only by brute force." Another group that was the target of genocidal policies in South-West Africa were the Nama, the only surviving relatively pure-blooded descendants of the Khoikhoi or "Hottentots" who had occupied most of southern Africa before the great Bantu migration. According to historian Helmut Bley, "Not only did the German official deliberately intend to wipe out the Nama race, but the majority of the settlers believed that the Nama were useless in the widest sense of the term, and that there was no further point in preserving the race."[21]

It is tempting to see the genocidal brutality of the German officials and settlers in South-West Africa as reflective of a peculiar mind-set that would later sanction the annihilation of European Jewry. Perhaps Hannah Arendt was right, at least in the German case, when she postulated that the seeds of totalitarianism were sown during the colonial experience in Africa.[22] It needs to be noted, in all fairness, however, that word of the order to exterminate the Hereros aroused sufficient protest in Germany itself to oblige the government in Berlin to disallow it, although it did so too tardily and ambiguously to prevent the genocide from taking place.[23] But the often overlooked tragedy of German colonialism in southern Africa shows that pre-Nazi German racism was not directed exclusively at Jews. Hitler's view of blacks as *Untermenschen* was not exceptional. The history of German colonialism also suggests that "final solutions" to the "problems" created by ethnoracial groups considered useless or dangerous were acceptable to at least some Germans as early as 1904 and 1905.

The German Jews themselves enjoyed a temporary respite from flagrant expressions of political antisemitism during the period between the late 1890s and World War I, partly because the attention of racial chauvinists and *völkisch* nationalists was directed outward rather than inward. This era saw the demise of the antisemitic parties and the incorporation of antisemitism into the rhetoric of the Conservative Party and the Pan-German League as a theme subsidiary to the main emphasis on the pursuit of national prestige and power on the world stage. But this hiatus did not mean that Jews were immune from prejudice and discrimination. Antisemitism continued to function as a "cultural code" limiting the access of Jews to many realms of German associational and professional life, even though politicians were invoking it less often.[24] So long as Germany's ambition to be a dominant world power seemed on the way to being fulfilled, there was no strong incentive to make Jews scapegoats for national failure. But the basic attitudes that would make Jews the most likely target of a search for the inner sources of a German defeat and humiliation were already in place.

World War I had a great impact on group relations in all three of the countries that had developed or would develop overtly racist regimes. A significant indirect result was its bringing an end to the age of Western imperial expansion that had provided a context for the legitimization of racial Darwinism. W.E.B. Du Bois may have exaggerated somewhat when he attributed the Great War primarily to the rivalries created by the scramble for Africa.[25] But the heavy cost of the conflict in life and treasure put a damper on the pursuit of new possessions, at least until Italy invaded Ethiopia in 1936. Germany's African dependencies were added to the colonial empires of England, France, and the self-governing commonwealth of South Africa under the League of Nations mandate system, which raised the possibility of eventual self-government. Furthermore, the Wilsonian slogan of "self-determination" helped to inspire fledgling independence movements in many colonies. Actual decolonization would not occur until after another even more devastating world war, but by the 1920s Western nations had already lost much of the will and capacity to maintain extensive overseas empires.

Being on the winning side and only marginally or belatedly involved in the European conflict, the United States and South Africa were much less directly affected by the war than was the loser, Germany. Nevertheless, the war and its consequences significantly altered black-white relations in both countries. Labor shortages caused by the war-induced decline of immigration from Europe in 1914 inspired the Great Migration of African Americans from the rural South to the urban North that persisted into the postwar years and nationalized a social issue that had previously been regarded as a regional problem. Black soldiers, who had fought in segregated units in France, returned seeking renewed respect because of their contributions to the Allied victory, only to encounter riots, lynch mobs, and a revived Ku Klux Klan. But the militancy associated with the "New Negro" and Garvey movements of the 1920s convinced many whites—especially in the North, where blacks had greater freedom of expression—that the southern image of the "happy darky" was false. The growth of a more sympathetic attitude toward blacks was reflected in white patronage of the National Association for the Advancement of Colored People, which had been founded in 1909, and in the rise of a school of anthropologists led by Franz Boas that attributed group differences primarily to culture, rather than biological race, and also refrained from ranking ethnoracial groups. Between 1917 and 1939 a series of Supreme Court decisions chipped away at the edifice of segregation, curbing, for example, legal enforcement of residential segregation and the denial to blacks of access to state-financed postgraduate education.

Prominent among the liberal interracialists of the interwar years were Jewish immigrants like Boas who could identify with the victims of racism because of their own experiences with European antisemitism. Changing white attitudes reflected to some extent a growth in black political power. The shift of African American population from the South to the North made blacks once again voters. By the 1930s, they were numerous enough to decide close elections in some major cities and pivotal industrial states, and the Democrats welcomed them into their urban/ethnic coalitions. In the South, however, conditions remained virtually unchanged in the postwar years. The new political clout of northern blacks and the enhanced power of the federal government as a result of the New Deal had yet to be translated into an assault on the Jim Crow system, which was still sustained by the constitutional doctrine of states' rights and the southern Democratic Party's wholehearted commitment to white supremacy.

In South Africa a substantial migration of blacks from the countryside to the cities during and after the Great War was also accompanied by an increase in the extent and intensity of African protest politics. But rather than an enhancement of black power and a mellowing of white attitudes, something like the reverse occurred. "Influx controls" on migrants, along with confinement to segregated townships or compounds of those who received permission to remain in urban-industrial areas, set the basic pattern for the system of labor coercion that would be fully and ruthlessly implemented during the apartheid era. The interwar period was one of increasing repression and denial of rights, culminating in 1936 when all Africans were removed from the common voters' roll in the Cape Province.[26] The debate among whites was not over the necessity for segregation but only on the details of its implementation. Relatively liberal white intellectuals and academics used the new cultural anthropology not to promote inclusion of blacks, as Boas did in the United States, but rather as a sophisticated defense of group separation, one that substituted cultural integrity for racial purity as the aim of the policy.[27] During the 1920s, working-class whites were given a measure of security against black competition much greater than that enjoyed by poor whites in the American South after the abolition of slavery. The passage in 1924 and thereafter of new laws protecting "civilized labor" and erecting "industrial color bars" pegged the wages of whites at artificially high levels and gave them exclusive access to skilled jobs and other kinds of desirable employment. In 1936 the South African parliament closed a glaring loophole in the developing system of racial differentiation and separation when, for the first time, it prohibited marriage between whites and Africans.

World War I and its aftermath was of course a much more shattering and demoralizing experience for Germans than it was for white Americans and South Africans. The fact that Germany agreed to humiliating and debilitating peace terms without actually being invaded and conquered made the outcome an exceedingly bitter pill for militarists and nationalists. The legitimacy of the Weimar Republic was in question from the moment of its establishment. The insistence of the victors on the full payment of reparations, leading in 1923 to the French occupation of the Ruhr and the subsequent hyperinflation, further discredited the government and the liberal principles on which it was based. As insecurity and dishonor turned into panic and desperation, the Nazi Party, organized in 1921, emerged as one response to the crisis. The history of the fall of the Weimar Republic and Adolph Hitler's rise to power has been told many times. For our purposes, it suffices to reemphasize the role of antisemitism.[28]

No careful reader of *Mein Kampf*, written in 1924 while Hitler was in prison after the failure of the "beer hall *putsch*" in Munich in 1923, can doubt that hatred and fear of the Jews was the main obsession behind the political movement that he led and personified. The text manifests the sincerity of the fanatic more than the cant of the demagogue whenever Hitler is referring to "the Jewish menace" (although the authenticity of his "socialist" commitment to the economic welfare of the working classes might be questioned). Jews were responsible, in Hitler's eyes, for Germany's loss of the war, its collapsing economy, and the threat posed to it by the Russian Revolution and the rise of Bolshevism. The vast Jewish conspiracy that Hitler imagined was responsible for the threat coming from two seemingly conflicting sources—international capitalism and Soviet Communism— both of which were antithetical to what he conceived of as the German national soul, or *Volksgeist*. Jews stood for all varieties of internationalism, cosmopolitanism, and universalism. They were leading practitioners and promoters of the transnational modern art that Hitler, the onetime painter, believed was corrupting the aesthetic standards of the West. To the internationalism of the Jews, Hitler opposed the nationalism of the Germans, which was based squarely on race.[29]

For Hitler, as for secular antisemites since the time of Marr and Dühring, Jews (like Germans) were ultimately defined not by religion or ethnicity but by biological race. But Hitler managed to synthesize the mystical tradition of *völkisch* nationalism with the new scientific racism inspired by the eugenics movement. He and his disciples also transcended the antimodernism of early antisemitic thinkers by embracing advanced technology when it was in the service of the German *Volksgeist* and not the Jewish "money power." This was the ideology that Jeffrey Herf has aptly called "reactionary modernism."[30] But Hitler's image of the Jew also included a strong whiff of the ancient folk tradition that imagined Jews to be minions of the Devil. They were not merely biologically unfit but incurably malevolent; the evil they represented was as much of the soul as of the body.[31]

In a famous passage Hitler revealed the following nightmare vision:

> With satanic joy in his face, the black-haired Jewish youth lurks in wait for the unsuspecting girl whom he defiles with his blood, thus stealing her from her people. With every means he seeks to destroy the racial foundations of the people he has set out to subjugate. Just as he himself systematically ruins women, he does not shrink from pulling down the blood barriers for others, even on a large scale. It was and it is Jews who bring the Negroes into the Rhineland, always with the same secret thought and clear aim of ruining the hated white race by the necessarily resulting bastardization, throwing it down from its

cultural and political height, and himself rising to be its master.[32]

This text reveals more about the deep sources of extreme racism than almost any that could be found. The lynch mobs of the American South often justified their atrocities by alleging the rape or attempted rape of white women by black men. The fear of sexual pollution or violation by the allegedly subhuman race is close to the heart of murderous or genocidal racism whenever and wherever it appears. In the racist imagination, blacks have been somewhat more likely than Jews to be viewed as violent sexual predators. The myth of the oversized black penis may be contrasted with the turn-of-the-century antisemitic belief that the large Jewish nose signified a *small* penis, further truncated by circumcision. Such images raised questions about Jewish masculinity or virility.[33] But the villainous eighteenth-century "Court Jew" in Viet Harlan's 1940 film *Jew Süss* manages to rape a woman from a prominent Christian family and is lynched as a result.[34] The notion of the Jew as a cunning seducer, and occasionally a violent rapist, was a staple of Nazi propaganda. In the passage warning against "the black-haired Jewish youth" Hitler also manages to arouse fears of black sexuality when he blames the Jews for the introduction into the Rhineland of soldiers from the French African colonies, some of whom had affairs with German women that resulted in children of mixed ancestry. A Negrophobic white supremacist as well as a racist antisemite, the future *Führer* identified the principle of racial equality being promulgated by Jews and Marxists with "a bastardized and niggerized world" in which "all concepts of the humanly beautiful and sublime, as well as all ideas of an idealized future of our humanity, would be lost forever."[35] Hitler even claimed that the French toleration of black-white intermarriage and its seemingly color-blind conception of assimilation was turning France into an extension of Africa into the heartland of Europe.[36]

Like everyone else who was threatening German nationality and racial purity, the French were of course doing the bidding of the Jews—the ultimate enemy. At no point in *Mein Kampf* does Hitler explicitly call for the extermination of the Jews, but the implication that they would have no place in a resurgent and regenerated Germany is unmistakable. Furthermore, given the fact that they were able to use nations like France and Russia as tools of their diabolical conspiracy, full security and fulfillment for Germany would be guaranteed only if all the Jews in the world were eliminated or at least rendered powerless. Something like the Holocaust was not an illogical or far-fetched consequence of such thinking. Something more than, or different from, simple biological racism may be required for an understanding of Hitler's phobic antisemitism and that of some of his followers. In the statement he dictated to Martin Bormann shortly before his death in 1945, he called the Jews "more than anything else, a community of the spirit . . . with a sort of relationship with destiny." Their "trait of not being able to assimilate . . . defines the race and must be reluctantly accepted as a triumph of the 'spirit' over the flesh."[37] If Hitler's racism had a nonmaterial or "spiritual" foundation, it would have been quite consistent with the beliefs of Alfred Rosenberg, the chief ideologist of the Nazi Party from the time that he stood in for Hitler when the latter went to prison in 1924. Italicized in Rosenberg's writings are adages like the following: *"Soul means race viewed from within: And vice versa, race is the externalization of Soul"* and *"The life of a race does not represent a logically-developed philosophy nor even the unfolding of a pattern according to law, but rather the development of a mystical synthesis, an activity of soul."*[38] Hitler and Rosenberg may not have literally believed in the Devil, but their sense of the malignant spiritual power that Jews could exert depended on a nonrational belief in supernatural agency as much as, if not more than, on the findings of racially biased biologists and eugenicists.

More amazing than the fact that a paranoid and delusional heterophobe like Hitler could find others who were prone to see the world in the same way was his success in making himself the absolute dictator of a modern and seemingly enlightened Western nation. I will not try to resolve the vexed question of how much direct responsibility the German people as a whole bear for the Nazi assault on the Jews. Neither of the extreme views—that Hitler and a few of his closest followers bear all of the guilt or that the ordinary German was a potentially homicidal Jew-hater— seems plausible to me.[39] Saul Friedlander, the foremost American authority on Nazi Germany and the Jews, notes that Hitler's appeal was broad and varied, that he offered solutions to problems afflicting various sectors of German society. (Indeed one thing that gave his movement a broader appeal than those drawing exclusively on the antisemitism of the economically conservative members of the middle class was that he professed sympathy for workers being exploited by ruthless capitalists and promised to address their grievances.) His international and domestic achievements of the mid-1930s—putting Germans back to work, building the autobahn, occupying the Rhineland, staging and winning the Olympics—created the "unshaken faith" in him that "brought with it widespread acceptance, passive or not, of the measures against the Jews."[40] Antisemitic policies thus became part of a package that could be accepted only in its totality.

This does not mean, however, that ordinary Germans were unlikely to harbor antisemitic sentiments. A belief in the ineradicable Otherness of the Jew had become firmly rooted in German culture as a result of decades, if not centuries, of antisemitic discourse.[41] But such prejudice can be of relatively low intensity and does not automatically lead to overtly racist regimes or holocausts. Hitler and the Nazi leadership were the instigators and implementers of the persecutions of the 1930s and the exterminations of the war years. What they required from most Germans was acquiescence rather than direct involvement. They would not have received it, however, if Jews had been accepted as fellow members of the national community, or *Volksgemeinschaft*.

From the time they came to power in 1933, the Nazis harassed and abused Germany's half-million Jews. But it was with the passage of the Nuremberg Laws in 1935 that Germany became a full-fledged racist regime, comparable to those already established in the American South or coming into existence in South Africa. One of the laws limited German citizenship to those who were of German or related ancestry, which excluded all Jews. (Blacks in the American South were nominally citizens, but the rights associated with citizenship had been effectively nullified.) German Jews thus became resident aliens in the land of their birth. Another law prohibited marriage and sexual relations between Jews and German citizens. American laws against marriage between whites and people of color, then on the books in a majority of the states, were the main foreign precedents for such legislation.[42] (As we have seen, South Africa did not begin to outlaw miscegenation until 1936.) It is of comparative interest, however, that the Nazi definition of a Jew was never as stringent as "the one-drop rule" that prevailed in the categorization of Negroes in the race-purity laws of the American South. To be automatically Jewish, one had to have three Jewish grandparents. (Because many Jews, especially those with forebears who had married Germans, lacked physical characteristics distinctive enough to distinguish them from Aryans, religious affiliation had to serve as a surrogate for biological race in the probing of ancestry.) Those who were one-fourth or even one-half Jewish in ancestry (*Mischlinge*) could be considered German citizens if they did not practice Judaism or marry Jews or other part-Jews. Allowing quarter-Jews to marry full-blooded Germans, the Nazis concluded, would not pollute the nation's bloodstream to an intolerable degree. But half-Jews were in practice allowed to marry only Jews.[43] To this limited extent, therefore, German antisemitism was less rigorous in its attitude toward "racial purity" than was American white supremacy. It was, however, more consistent in its abhorrence of miscegenation; unlike the American states, it banned extramarital interracial sex as well as intermarriage. The apartheid regime in South Africa would follow the Nazi example with its Immorality Act of 1949.

Unlike racist regimes in the American South of the Jim Crow era and during South Africa's transition from "native segregation" to apartheid, the Nazi version did not evolve out of a preexisting racial order based on slavery or colonial-style domination. In fact the assault on the Jews was the act of a revolutionary totalitarian regime that brought radical changes in many areas, not just in Jewish-gentile relations. Although Jews had certainly been discriminated against before 1935, the Nuremberg Laws categorically transformed their status. As the existence of many *Mischlinge* suggests, the rate of German-Jewish intermarriage before the Nazi era had been relatively high, whereas American and South African antimiscegenation laws outlawed a practice that was quite rare. (The proportion of Jews marrying non-Jews had in fact risen from almost 8 percent in the period 1901–1904 to just under 23 percent in 1929.)[44] The revolutionary process did not stop with the denial of citizenship and the banning of intermarriage. After the officially sponsored *Kristallnacht* pogrom of 1938, the public segregation of Jews was carried to extremes that in some respects went beyond Jim Crow and apartheid (for example, all access to public transportation was denied to Jews, their children could no longer attend school, a special curfew was imposed upon them, and they could shop only during certain hours). In 1939, Jews were denied the right to operate businesses and possess substantial property. The aim now was not simply the subordination of Jews but their elimination through forced emigration, or, if that failed, internment in concentration camps that could become death camps. The fact that Nazi Germany in the 1930s was on the path from being merely an overtly racist regime to being a deliberately genocidal one distinguishes it quite sharply from the American and South African cases.[45]

Nazi racism of course applied to all non-Aryans and not simply the Jews. Proclamations implementing the Nuremberg Laws put Gypsies in the same pariah category as Jews, and a substantial portion of them were placed in concentration camps within Germany in 1936, from which some would eventually be sent East to die in the gas chambers of Auschwitz. But, as a recent study has shown, much confusion existed on the precise racial status of Gypsies, and apparently no clear decision was ever made to exterminate them as a race. It was the belief of Gestapo chief Heinrich Himmler that "racially pure" Gypsies were direct descendants of the ancient Aryans and should be preserved as subjects of ethnological research into the early development of the contemporary "master race." Consequently, only Gypsy *"Mischlinge"* were sent to Auschwitz. Whereas Jews of mixed descent were for a time treated with somewhat greater leniency than full Jews, the opposite preference operated in relation to Gypsies.[46] As for the hundreds of mixed offspring sired on German women by French colonial African soldiers in the Rhineland during the early postwar years, they were rounded up and sterilized in 1937, thus saving German blood from an intolerable source of pollution.[47] Had there been a significant black population in Germany, they might conceivably have been sent to gas chambers along with all the Jews who could be apprehended and some of the Gypsies. Nevertheless, the German fixation on the Jews clearly did not depend on large numbers: they were only about 1 percent of the population when Hitler came to power. What it did reflect was the belief that they were the enemy inside the gates, gnawing at the vitals of the German nation on behalf of the worldwide Jewish conspiracy that lay behind both Bolshevism and international finance capitalism. Despite their much greater relative numbers, blacks in the southern United States and South Africa were of economic value and, after Jim Crow and "native segregation" were firmly in place, were not usually seen as constituting an imminent threat to white domination.

The Second World War, into which Hitler plunged the world, was the climax and turning point in the history of racism in the twentieth century. It, and the Cold War that followed quickly on its heels, revolutionized the context within which groups thought of as "races" confronted each other and interacted. Events in the 1940s and 1950s would establish patterns of thought and action concerning race and racism that would endure for the rest of the century. The specific results of the war that most shaped attitudes toward race were the Holocaust and the beginnings of decolonization in Asia and Africa. The first aroused widespread soul-searching and moral revulsion by revealing what happened when extreme racism was carried to its logical outcome. The second eventually gave geopolitical significance to many newly independent nations that were composed of people whose skin color made them abhor and denounce the persistence of white supremacy.

The events of the Holocaust are too well known to bear repeating here. It is the reaction of the Western world to the Nazis' murder of six million Jews that is most germane to our subject. A milder form of antisemitism had made countries like the United States and Great Britain reluctant to accept many Jewish refugees from Germany before the outbreak of the war, and it was hard for them to believe the first accounts of "the final solution" that appeared in 1942–1943. But the horrible truth revealed by the liberation of the death camps in 1945 could not be evaded. The resulting shock and mortification did more to discredit racism—at least in its blatant ideological forms—than had any previous historical event. As a consequence of the Allied victory over the Nazis in World War II, according to the German philosopher Jürgen Habermas, "the rug was pulled out from under *all* claims to legitimacy that did not at least rhetorically embrace the universalistic spirit of the political Enlightenment."[48] What the Nazis had done was so indefensible that later neo-Nazis would deny that the Holocaust had taken place rather than try to justify it.

The eugenics movement, which had enjoyed scientific respectability in the United States and Britain before the war, did not survive the revelations of what the Nazis had done in its name. Not all eugenicists had been racists or even social conservatives, but the whole notion of using the state to improve the human gene pool was under a dark cloud for several decades after the war. The empirical genetic science of 1950 was not very different from that in 1940, when the possibility that there were innate differences between races, and that crossing them might have deleterious consequences, was still a respectable hypothesis. But in 1950 most prominent geneticists and physical anthropologists endorsed all or part of the UNESCO statement declaring that science gave no support to the notion that human groups differed in "their innate capacity for intellectual and emotional development" and that there was "no reliable evidence that disadvantageous effects are produced" by race crossing. The most important reason for the repudiation of eugenic racism, one prominent geneticist concluded, was "the revulsion of educated people in the United States and England to Nazi race doctrines and their use in justifying the extermination of the Jews."[49]

Within the United States, there was a growing realization among those concerned with international relations that Jim Crow not only was analogous to Nazi treatment of the Jews and thus morally indefensible but was also contrary to the national interest. The Commission to Study the International Organization of the Peace reported in 1944 that "the cancerous Negro situation in our country gives fodder to enemy propaganda and makes our ideals stick like dry bread in the throat. . . . Through revulsion against Nazi doctrines, we may, however, hope to speed up the process of bringing our own practices in each nation more in conformity with our professed ideals."[50] During the same year, Gunnar Myrdal endorsed such hopes in his seminal study of black-white relations in the United States, *An American Dilemma*: "The War is crucial for the future of the Negro, and the Negro problem is crucial in the War. There is bound to be a redefinition of the Negro's status in America as a result of this War." It was a central theme of his book that *not since Reconstruction has there been more reason to anticipate fundamental changes in American race relations, changes which will involve a development toward the American ideals.*[51]

The conjunction of the Cold War and the decolonization of Asia and Africa created enormous practical incentives for racial reform in the United States. Statesmen, policy makers, molders of public opinion, and even judges became increasingly sensitive during the postwar years to the international liability of America's racial practices in the struggle with the Soviet Union for the "hearts and minds" of people in what came to be known as the Third World.[52] The Communists had some natural advantages in this conflict. Marxist ideology was insistently "nonracialist"; the various non-European nationalities in the Soviet Union were, on paper at least, equal under the law; and blacks from the West who visited Russia could be entertained in a manner that seemed to demonstrate a total absence of color prejudice. During the early Cold War, the Soviets gained an enormous propaganda advantage in calling attention to America's practice of segregation and to the incidents of racial violence and terrorism that continued to occur in the southern states. When several of Europe's African colonies became independent in the late 1950s and early 1960s, discrimination against African diplomats in Washington, D.C., and the surrounding area became a major embarrassment for the State Department that helped to provoke some of the earliest federal efforts toward the desegregation of public facilities.[53]

The geopolitical costs of the persistence of legalized racism in the United States were high enough to raise the question of why it took two full decades from the end of World War II and the onset of the Cold War for Congress to pass the civil rights legislation that outlawed Jim Crow and gave protection to black voting rights. Indeed, it was not until 1967 that a Supreme Court decision nullified the last state laws enshrining the central symbol of a racist regime—the ban on intermarriage. Part of the explanation for the delay can be found in the popular association of "forced desegregation" with Communism during the heyday of McCarthyism in the late '40s and early '50s.[54] But a full answer would have to take into account some combination of entrenched racist beliefs and the protection that the federal system continued to provide for the deviation of the southern states from the national norm of legal equality.

An important recent study has argued that the progress of racial equality in the United States has been fostered mainly by the external pressures generated by wars and international rivalries. In times when national success or survival seems to depend on inclusiveness and the affirmation of egalitarian values, Philip A. Klinkner and Rogers M. Smith argue in *The Unsteady March*, the extension of rights to African Americans has been possible. When such pressures have been absent, reversion to the seemingly normal pattern of racial inequality has taken place. World War II and the Cold War thus provided a window of opportunity for blacks that is now closing.[55] There is much evidence to support such a view of African American history. At best progress has meant two steps forward and one step backward from the time that the wake of the American Revolution abolished slavery in the North but strengthened it in the South. Significant progress has occurred, however: legalized segregation is as dead today as racial slavery was in 1865. An exclusive emphasis on reasons of state as the motivation for egalitarian reform risks overlooking the moral dimension—the extent to which racism conflicts with other values that Americans are supposed to hold. The national conscience is admittedly easier to arouse when self-interest can also be invoked. But to the considerable extent that the Holocaust made blatant racism of all kinds morally disreputable, African Americans and other traditional or potential victims of racial discrimination, not only in the United States but throughout the world, gained a measure of international sympathy and even protection. The United Nations' Universal Declaration of Human Rights and Convention on the Prevention and Punishment of the Crime of Genocide did not prevent the occurrence of racial injustice or even the mass murder of racial or ethnic Others, but it increased the chance that something might be done about violations of what were now international norms.[56]

The one overtly racist regime that survived World War II and the Cold War was the South African, which did not in fact come to maturity until the victory of the Afrikaner-dominated Nationalist Party in 1948 ushered in the era of apartheid. Most of the Nationalist leaders who later came to power opposed going to war with Germany in 1939, and some remained sympathetic to the Nazi regime throughout the conflict. Antisemitism of the populist, anticapitalist variety had been a secondary theme in Afrikaner Nationalist polemics in the 1930s, but the postwar party, for the most part, eschewed attacking Jews per se as either capitalists or communists. The campaign against the *svart gevaar* (black menace) in 1948 put the English-speaking Jews on the right side of the color line, even if they were not part of the *Volk*. Not wishing to be associated with the Holocaust and seeking to establish ties of mutual advantage with Israel, the architects of apartheid concentrated on justifying white rule in southern Africa.[57]

Decolonization and the Cold War influenced South African race policy in ways that were almost diametrically opposed to how they affected black-white relations in the United States. Since South Africa was a prime example of white settler rule over an indigenous majority, it was precluded from riding the bandwagon of decolonization (as the United States tried to present itself as doing) except in a transparently deceitful way. As more and more African countries became independent and the ring of "frontline states" grew closer and closer to South Africa's borders, determination to maintain white supremacy grew. The ace in the hole that South Africa's leaders believed they possessed at the height of the Cold War was the role they thought they could play as a bastion of anticommunism on a continent endangered by the red menace. On that basis they could expect Western aid and tacit support—which in fact they received in relative abundance between the late '40s and the late '70s. It is a supreme irony that the Truman administration, which did much to foster the movement for civil rights for African Americans, also gave aid and comfort to the new apartheid regime in the belief that its treatment of Africans was tolerable so long as it stood with "the free world" against Soviet Communism.[58]

South Africa after 1948 designed and constructed the most comprehensive racist regime meant to be a permanent structure that the world has ever seen. (The architects of the Nazi regime of course viewed their handiwork as the process that would lead to a society in which there would be no racial distinctions because there would be only one race.) Building on the earlier pattern of "native segregation," the makers of apartheid denied to Africans, more than 70 percent of the total population, the right to reside permanently outside of the rural "homelands" or "Bantustans" that added up to about 13 percent of the total land area of South Africa. Those permitted to reside in urban and industrial areas were treated as resident aliens or guest workers whose sole function was to serve the economic interests of the whites. The fiction of the African as cultural alien or purely ethnic Other was used to mask the essential racism of the regime. In 1952 Prime Minister J. G. Strydom gave an honest answer to the question of what apartheid was all about: "Our policy," he forthrightly announced, "is that the Europeans must stand their ground and remain *Baas* [master] in South Africa. If we reject the *Herrenvolk* idea . . . if the franchise is to be extended to non-Europeans, and if non-Europeans are developed on the same basis as Europeans, how can the Europeans remain *Baas*? Our view is that in every sphere the Europeans must retain the right to rule the country and to keep it a white man's country."[59] But such frank defenses of white supremacy were obfuscated by an ideological fog under Strydom's successor, Hendrik Verwoerd, who sought desperately to give a compelling philosophical, moral, and theological rationale for what Strydom had in effect conceded was simply group selfishness.

In the late 1950s, in an unconvincing effort to identify South Africa with the seemingly irresistible decolonization movement, Verwoerd held out the prospect of "independence" for the African homelands, and four of them eventually accepted the offer of a nominal autonomy that the outside world refused to recognize. The mature ideology of apartheid, as formulated by Verwoerd and a group of

Afrikaner academics and intellectuals (many of whom had studied in Germany before the war), was to adapt the romantic nationalism of Herder and Fichte to the South African case. At the same time, pro-apartheid theologians searched the Scriptures for an expression of the divine will that would sanction South Africa's race policies in the face of growing condemnation from much of the rest of Christendom. Although some early advocates of apartheid followed the Nazi example of synthesizing *völkisch* nationalism and biological racism, the defenders of apartheid who responded to international criticism between the 1950s and the 1970s eschewed biological arguments in favor of what the historian Saul DuBow has aptly described as "cultural essentialism."[60]

The basic idea, which could have come directly from Herder, was that each *Volk* was programmed to develop a unique and worthy culture. But to do so, it had to be protected from contamination by other cultures; this required a significant degree of isolation and "separate development." For Afrikaners, "Christian Nationalism" meant schools and universities, separate from those attended by the English, in which the language and values of the Afrikaner *Volk* could flower. In theory, it meant the same thing for Zulus and Xhosa, whose homelands would be the cradles for the growth of their own unique national cultures. The identification of language, culture, and race that had been characteristic of early German nationalist thinking was revivified without the stress on the purely biological or genetic factor that Nazis had given it. Theologians of the South African Dutch Reformed Church found their scriptural warrant, not in the Curse of Ham that had served

some of their slaveholding ancestors, but in the story of
the destruction of the Tower of Babel. In their exegesis of
this tale, the religious apologists for apartheid identified a
God who regarded attempts to unify the human race as
manifestations of sinful pride. As a remedy to the evils of
universalism, he prescribed a strict division of humanity
into separate linguistic and cultural groups, which were
commanded, in effect, to keep their distance from each
other and to "develop along their own lines."[61] If we were
to take these ideologues at their word, cultural relativism
rather than hierarchical racism would have to be acknowledged as the essence of apartheid.

Their word, however, cannot obscure the extent to
which the practice of apartheid belied these principles and
reflected the unvarnished *Herrenvolk* ideology of J. G. Strydom, who affirmed that it was his "color sense" that was
the key to the white man's survival in South Africa.[62] Color
clearly trumped culture when it came to the differential
privileges that all "Europeans," whatever their language
and ethnicity, enjoyed in contrast to all "nonwhites," whose
unique linguistic or cultural characteristics did not prevent
them from being consigned to separate facilities for *"nie
blankes."* The long struggle of Afrikaners for economic, social, and cultural parity with the English was won relatively
easily once they had the full power of the state at their
disposal after 1948. Increasingly the "we" became all whites
and the "they" became all Africans or even all nonwhites.

The "Coloreds"—a substantial population group of
mixed origin that had developed in the Western Cape out
of the interaction of Europeans, East Asians, Khoikhoi
("Hottentots"), and black Africans in the seventeenth and

eighteenth centuries—were substantially Afrikaans in language and culture. But during the apartheid era they were increasingly segregated and discriminated against. By the 1960s they found themselves reduced from a status intermediate between whites and Africans to one that was closer to the latter than to the former. The Immorality, Group Marriage, and Urban Areas Acts, which were among the earliest apartheid laws, made it for the first time illegal for Coloreds to have sex, intermarry, or live in the same neighborhoods with whites. Only an explicit and straightforward racism could justify these policies, as some of the more principled advocates of "ideal apartheid" recognized. But the official culturalist rationale can also be considered racist if we accept the notion that the essence of racism is not biological determinism per se but the positing, on whatever basis, of unbridgeable differences between ethnic or descent groups—distinctions that are then used to justify their differential treatment. Even if Coloreds had been admitted, as some consistent cultural nationalists advocated, into the bosom of the Afrikaner *Volk*, South Africa would still have had an overtly racist regime as far as Africans were concerned. The division of blacks into pseudonations did not reflect a genuine cultural pluralism but was rather the divide-and-conquer strategy of a ruling minority.[63]

If the demise of Jim Crow can be attributed partially to strategic considerations arising from the Cold War, the end of that conflict contributed significantly to the death of apartheid. When the South African regime could no longer expect aid or even toleration from the West for its role in the defense of capitalism, and the disintegrating Soviet Union cut off aid to the African National Congress, the two sides in the struggle went to the bargaining table to resolve a conflict in which neither could anticipate total victory.[64]

The fact that the negotiations led to the one result that white leaders had said for decades that they would never accept—one person, one vote—was in the first instance an achievement of Nelson Mandela's adroit bargaining skills. But the release of Mandela from prison, as well as the prestige and moral stature that he brought to the negotiations, resulted in large part from an aroused international public opinion. The moral condemnation of the world and the economic sanctions to which it eventually gave rise undermined the willingness of white South Africans to defend apartheid at all costs. By the late 1980s, it had apparently become psychologically demoralizing and economically costly to be the "polecat of the world." The revulsion against official racism that inspired the international campaign to free Mandela and end apartheid can be traced ultimately to the antiracist fallout from the Holocaust, activated and reinforced in relation to people of color by the success of decolonization and the civil rights movements elsewhere in the world during the decades immediately after the war. South Africa's policies were too reminiscent of Nazi Germany's to escape the opprobrium that was now associated with overtly racist regimes, and its harsh practice of a peculiar internal form of colonialism put it at odds with a world of independent nations that had replaced the European colonial empires.

—

Racism at the Dawn
of the Twenty-First Century

It is widely believed that racism remains a major international problem at the dawn of the twenty-first century. The term is used in some countries and in some circles to describe hostility and discrimination directed against a group for virtually any reason. The French, for example, sometimes use the term to describe biases founded on age, gender, or sexual orientation. Usually, however, the act of racializing the Other seizes upon differences that are "ethnic" in some sense. According to political scientist Donald L. Horowitz, ethnicity "is based on a myth of collective ancestry, which usually carries with it traits believed to be innate. Some notion of ascription, however diluted, and affinity deriving from it are inseparable from the concept of ethnicity."[1] The marks or identifiers usually associated with ethnicity are language, religion, customs, and physical characteristics (inborn or acquired). One or more (sometimes all) may serve as sources of ethnic divisiveness; any one of them can provoke disdain, discrimination, or violence on the part of another group that does not share the trait or traits that have come to define ethnic Otherness. It is justifiable, as I once did in an essay, to describe the essence of racism as ethnicity made hierarchical, or, in other words, making difference invidious and disadvantageous through the application of power.[2] But, as the preceding chapters of this book suggest, I would now put more stress than I did then on the presence and articulation of a belief that the defining traits are innate or unchangeable. Pigmentation, however, is not the only supposedly indelible mark of difference upon which racism can be based, as the history of antisemitism clearly demonstrates.

In September 2001 the United Nations sponsored a World Conference on Racism, Racial Discrimination, Xenophobia, and Related Intolerance in Durban, South Africa. This multiple terminology suggests that doubt may have existed as to whether the use of the term "racism" by itself was sufficient to denote all the hostilities and oppressions that concerned the conferees. In the introduction to this book I made distinctions between racism and xenophobia and between racial and religious intolerance. Xenophobia (literally the fear of strangers) is an ancient and virtually universal phenomenon, while racism, I have argued, is a historical construction with a traceable career covering the period between the fourteenth century and the twenty-first. Religious bigotry is directed at what people believe and not at what they are. Unlike "racial" characteristics, religious convictions are usually considered changeable by an act of will. (It is, however, useful to be reminded by Horowitz that for many groups outside the West, "religion is not a matter of faith but a given, an integral part of their identity, and for some an inextricable component of their sense of peoplehood.")[3] In the third chapter, I argued that racism has declined in the past half-century as a result of the Holocaust and the subsequent overthrow of Jim Crow in the United States and apartheid in South Africa. Does this mean that the UN conference can be viewed as a kind of valedictory to an "age of racism," and that we can anticipate a new century without the kind of hatreds and injustices that have characterize the old one? Is racism only, or soon to be only, history?

Unfortunately racism survives even in the carefully delineated sense that has governed this study of its history. The Holocaust and decolonization may have permanently discredited what I have called "overtly racist regimes," but this good news should not be inflated into a belief that racism itself is dead or even dying. As we saw in earlier chapters, group inequalities associated with what are taken to be indelible marks of inferior or unworthy ancestry can exist without having the full apparatus of the modern state to sustain them. We have also had the opportunity to observe situations in which ideologies that do not invoke race in the modern biological sense serve to rationalize caste systems or forms of exploitation that reflect the essentially racist vision of indelible, unbridgeable, and invidious differences between human groups. What has been called "the new racism" in the United States, Great Britain, and France is a way of thinking about difference that reifies and essentializes culture rather than genetic endowment, or in other words makes culture do the work of race.[4] The arrival of large numbers of immigrants from former colonies in England and France has encouraged the use of "culture" as a way of distinguishing unwelcome newcomers for those who are genuinely "British" or "French." In Britain skin color and culture remain closely associated, and it is often assumed that ways of life are as unchangeable as pigmentation. In France color per se is less important; in theory dark-skinned or swarthy newcomers may be deemed acceptable if they show the desire and capacity to assimilate. But it is generally assumed that most of them cannot or will not assimilate to *la culture française* by sacrificing their preexisting ethnic and religious identities. The United States, traditionally a land of immigrants, may be better able than most European nations to deal with the cultural diversity created by immigration. But discrimination against African Americans is now being justified as "rational" because it may be an appropriate response to the "dysfunctional" subculture that has allegedly taken possession of the souls of many black folk. The adverse effect of negative stereotypes on African Americans is intensified by the fact that their pigmentation makes them so easily identifiable.[5]

There is another sense in which the discrediting of scientific racism and the revulsion against official or legalized discrimination have fallen short of achieving racial justice and equality. Histories of slavery, Jim Crow, apartheid, or colonization have left many members of previously stigmatized and legally disadvantaged groups in an economically and psychologically vulnerable situation, which may make it difficult for them to compete with those whose families and forebears have not had to undergo such shattering experiences. The blacks now in power in South Africa cannot, given the resources at their command, adequately compensate blacks for three and a half centuries of expropriation, exploitation, and deprivation to the extent that would be required to make them truly equal to the whites. The damage left behind by "overtly racist regimes" may also encourage antisocial or self-destructive behavior. The failures and "pathologies" that can result seem to confirm negative stereotypes about the group that persist despite the removal of the full ideological scaffolding that once sustained them. Justice Harry Blackmun put it succinctly in a United States Supreme Court decision of 1978 that upheld the principle of affirmative action: "[I]n order to get beyond racism, we must first take account of race. There is no other way. And in order to treat some persons equally, we must treat them differently. We cannot—we dare not—let the Equal Protection clause perpetuate racial supremacy."[6] It is not merely a matter of failing to eliminate the last remnants of an outworn and discredited set of ideas and practices. The legacy of the past racism directed at blacks in the United States is more like a bacillus that we have failed to destroy, a live germ that not only continues to make some of us ill but retains the capacity to generate new strains of a disease for which we have no certain cure.

Antisemitic racism also persists and, despite the Holocaust and the creation of the State of Israel, retains the capacity to do harm. Hate groups in many countries continue to believe in the Hitlerian myth that the world is threatened by a Jewish conspiracy. The World Wide Web is filled with their ranting. (In the United States, where hatred of blacks and hatred of Jews tend to go together in the psyches of ultraracists, African Americans are often portrayed on the Websites as the mindless tools of diabolically clever Jews plotting to destroy white Christian America.) In Germany, France, the United States, and several eastern European countries, Jews have been attacked, swastikas painted on synagogues, and Jewish cemeteries desecrated. For many years, the Arab governments that object vehemently to the State of Israel and its policies have sponsored the dissemination of classic antisemitic propaganda, including that notorious forgery *The Protocols of the Elders of Zion*.[7]

In the Western democracies antisemitism is officially deplored, and words or actions based on it are confined to fringe groups that operate outside the law or (except in Austria) to parties that are too small to have much chance of sharing power in the foreseeable future. But Jewish leaders in several countries fear that passive antisemitism remains widespread, and that circumstances can be imagined that would cause a resurgence of its more virulent manifestations. The actions of the State of Israel against the Palestinians have led to charges by the General Assembly of the United Nations that Zionism constitutes a form of racism. It is difficult to deny that Israel has at times been unjust and even brutal to the Palestinians in the occupied territories or even within Israel itself. But is this racism, or the product of a conflict that is truly based on culture and religion rather than on differing "bloodlines" or genetic constitutions?

As the capacious title of the UN conference suggests, the main problem of human relations in the world today may not be solely, or perhaps even principally, one of racism in the sense of the term used in this book. If racism is not dead, it is less intense and intellectually respectable than it was a century or even a half-century ago. But human beings continue to mistreat other human beings on the basis of their ethnic identities. In a sense we may have returned to the chronological starting point of this inquiry. Before "the invention of racism" Christians persecuted Jews and Muslims because of their beliefs and the behavior that was associated with them. The Crusades were not fought under the banner of white, Aryan, or Indo-European superiority or the divine right of the *Herrenvolk* to rule over lesser breeds. The conflicts were defined in what we would today call cultural rather than racial terms. Of course, as has been often shown in this study, the line between "culturalism" and racism is not difficult to cross. Culture and even religion can become essentialized to the point that they can serve as a functional equivalent of biological racism, as has to some extent occurred recently in the perception of blacks in the United States and Britain, and of Muslims in several predominantly Christian nations.[8]

But many of the most bitter and bloody ethnic conflicts of our time have not required the full racialization of the Other to become devastating. Most of the minorities throughout the world that are victimized by discrimination or violence appear to be differentiated from their oppressors more by authentic cultural or religious differences than by race in the genetic sense. Irish Catholics in Ulster, North African Muslims in France, Turks in Germany, Albanian Muslims in what remains of Yugoslavia, Bosnians under Serbian or Croatian rule, Chechens in Russia, Muslims, Sikhs, and Christians in India, Tamils in Sri Lanka, Buddhists in Chinese-ruled Tibet, and Palestinians in Israel (one could go on and on) are not generally conceived of by the relevant majorities in terms that are racial in the sense used in this study. They are identified by their beliefs and behavior—not, or at least not principally, by their physical appearance or ancestry. In all or most of these cases, religion is the most salient difference between persecutors and persecuted. In social scientific terminology, the differences are thus ethnic, yes, but primarily ethnoreligious rather than ethnoracial. At this point, however, a reader might well feel that it makes little or no practical difference whether the inhumanity of one *ethnos* against another is based on religious fanaticism or on alleged differences in genetic endowment. Stress on religion and absence of the ideological component of biological determinism do not prevent massacres, ethnic cleansing, denial of equal citizenship, and economic discrimination.[9] The temptation to follow the current tendency to expand the term "racism" to include xenophobia and persecution based on religious and cultural differences is indeed difficult to resist.

Were we to succumb to this catchall usage, however, we would be unable to appreciate the special features of the Western ideological racism described in this study, such as its close relationship to the enslavement and colonial domination of people of color and the way that its antisemitic embodiment reflected the trauma of capitalist modernization. As we look to the future, we might also fail to recognize that making religion the principal marker of difference has implications somewhat different from those generated by locating it in the blood or the genes. As was the case with early medieval Christianity's abuse of Jews and Muslims, religious intolerance normally has an escape hatch. Conversion is always a theoretical possibility and may actually occur in some cases, especially when there is intermarriage between members of different ethnoreligious groups. (To my knowledge, none of the contemporary loci of ethnic conflict or domination have generated the formal prohibitions on intermarriage that characterized the overtly racist regimes, but ordinarily one spouse or the other must convert.) If ethnoreligious differences are less rigid than ethnoracial ones, however, they may be more durable. In an incisive comparison of conflict in South Africa and Northern Ireland, the sociologist Hamish Dickie-Clark predicted accurately in 1976 that the formal racial divide in South Africa would be easier to overcome than the sectarian split in Ulster. He based his prognostication on the belief that "racist claims are open to rational and empirical refutation, whereas the claims made by sectarian religion are so deeply imbedded in the matrix of faith and other-worldly authority that they are not similarly open to logic and observation."[10] Although it takes much more than rational persuasion to overcome racism, the fact that its foundations are subject to empirical falsification does make it more fragile than the incontrovertible and unquestioning faith demanded by sectarian or fundamentalist religion. Along with the dissemination of the truth about human physical differences, the struggle against racism also requires that stigmatized groups have enforceable civil rights, political empowerment in proportion to their numbers, and equal opportunity in education and employment (which may require special efforts to compensate for disadvantages inherited from the past). If persisting racial prejudices and inequalities make the complete separation of race and state counterproductive, the first line of defense against militant sectarianism would seem to be a total separation of church and state. The high wall that the United States

Supreme Court has at times affirmed, despite constant threats from zealous members of the Protestant majority, might serve as a model for other religiously diverse nations. If the United States has for most of its history set a bad example in the area of race relations, it has established a relatively good record in its handling of the religious diversity resulting from immigration.[11]

Will the color line of the twentieth century therefore be replaced or overshadowed by the faith or creed lines of the twenty-first? Will conflicts more often take the form of jihads or crusades than movements for human rights or social justice? Many signs point in that direction. Racism, as we have seen, offers material and psychological rewards to an ethnic group that has the power and the will to dominate or eliminate another ethnic group that it defines as inherently different from itself in ways justifying the treatment it receives. The emotion to which it appeals is either contempt or fear, depending on whether the dominant group views the Other as under control and securely "in its place" or conceivably capable of competition or reprisal. Its essential context has been the rise of commercial and industrial capitalism, and its trigger has been the interests and anxieties aroused by that great historical transformation.

But in the twenty-first century, we confront a global capitalism that draws no color line, because it seeks customers and collaborators from every race. A de facto color line remains because the non-Europeans of the world are, as a result of slavery, colonialism, or a late start on the path of modernization, on the average poorer and more disadvantaged than people of white or European ancestry. But active racism is not necessary to maintain this "new world order," nor is it clear that conventional antiracism can do very much to change it. In this context militant sectarianism or religious tribalism can easily become the refuge of people whose sense of community and traditional ethical values are threatened.[12] There is no arguing with someone who believes that abortion is murder or that eating pork or slaughtering cattle is an offense in the eyes of God. But it is not dogmatic religion itself that creates ethnoreligious conflict or theocratic regimes. It is the politicization of faith and the effort to make others conform to beliefs they do not share that threaten the peace of the world and of many countries within it. The Taliban ruled Afghanistan in ways that much of the rest of the world found unacceptable. But there are many milder manifestations of combative and coercive religious zealotry. Israelis and Palestinians are willing to fight to the death over control of sacred sites. Although most Muslim immigrants to Europe are not potential terrorists and do not seek to impose their beliefs on others, Christians and secularists alike make them targets of suspicion and discrimination. In the United States, the religious right seeks to control the behavior of those who do not share its views of abortion, sexual orientation, sexual morality, or euthanasia. In some countries, such as India, conflict and discrimination arise from the direct confrontation of dogmatic religious faiths. In others—the United States being a conspicuous example—the fault lines may be between the combined forces of more than one variety of dogmatic religiosity and a coalition of tolerant ecumenicists and nonreligious humanists.

It would be premature to contend that trying to contain culture wars over spiritual or moral values should replace struggles against racial hatred and domination at the center of concern for those who seek a just and peaceful world. As has been suggested, religion easily becomes race in the twisted minds of racist skinheads in eastern Germany or the United States. What characterizes many of the perpetrators of violence against the Other (whether identified racially or religiously) is social marginality. The greatest danger of direct violence comes from those descended from privileged or at least securely settled groups who find themselves on the outside of the modern (or postmodern) world of communications technology, global financial markets, and bureaucratized nation-states. Alienation from the course of local or world development can provoke either racism or religious fanaticism, depending on the cultural and social situation. Grasping for one's identity in a world that threatens to reduce everyone who is not part of the elite to a low-paid worker or a consumer of cheap, mass-produced commodities creates a hunger for meaning and a sense of self-worth that can most easily be satisfied by consciousness of race or religion. Race offers less of a haven to the alienated and disenchanted than it once did, because of the worldwide campaign against it that was one of the great achievements of the twentieth century. But absolutist religion retains its appeal, and to the extent that it becomes militant and politicized, it has the potential to become the twenty-first century's principal source of intergroup conflict and aggression.

The Concept of Racism
in Historical Discourse

Although commonly used, "racism" has become a loaded and ambiguous term. Both sides in the current debate over affirmative action in the United States, for example, have used it to describe their opponents. It can mean either a lamentable absence of "color blindness" in an allegedly postracist age *or* insensitivity to past and present discrimination against groups that to be helped must be racially categorized. Once considered primarily a matter of belief or ideology, "racism" may now express itself in institutional patterns or social practices that have adverse effects on members of groups thought of as "races," even if a conscious belief that they are inferior or unworthy is absent. The term is clearly in danger of losing the precision needed to make it an analytical tool for historians and social scientists examining the relations among human groups or collectivities. But few would deny that we need, as a bare minimum, a strong expression to describe some horrendous acts of brutality and injustice that were clearly inspired by beliefs associated with the concept of race—the vilification, lynching, and segregation of African Americans in the South during the Jim Crow era; the Nazis' demonization and extermination of European Jewry; and the noncitizenship and economic servitude of South African blacks under apartheid.

These three clear-cut examples of racism in both theory and practice draw our attention to the fact that two kinds of people have been conspicuously victimized by this proclivity to denigrate and abuse others because of their physical characteristics, ancestry, and alleged spiritual deficiencies: people of color (especially blacks) and Jews. In the main body of this study I compare these two principal manifestations of racism and probe the connections between them. Insight into the genesis and context of this undertaking can perhaps be enhanced by a review of how previous scholarship, including my own, has dealt with racism as a historical subject—what meanings have been given to it and what lessons may be learned from this historiography about where we might go from here. In light of the multiple current meanings of the term, some historians and social scientists, including myself, have been tempted at times to exclude the word from our vocabularies. In the introduction to an early book on "white supremacy" in the United States and South Africa, "I concluded that racism is too ambiguous and loaded a term to describe my subject effectively."[1] In a recent essay, Loïc Wacquant, a prominent sociologist of race, advocates "forsaking once and for all the inflammatory and exceedingly ductile category of 'racism' save as a descriptive term referring to empirically analyzable doctrines and beliefs about 'race.'"[2]

Most historians of race and racism have in fact limited themselves to the study of racial doctrines and beliefs and would therefore be permitted by Wacquant to continue using the term. But it was in part the limitations of considering racism simply as a doctrine or set of ideas that encouraged me to substitute the term "white supremacy" to designate the white-over-black manifestation of it. I wanted to examine the relationship between the cultural aspects—racist attitudes, beliefs, and ideas—and structures and politics of racial domination. To put it another way, my interest was not merely in the history of ideas and attitudes but in the history of ideology in the broadest sense of that term. What also concerned me, therefore, was the relationship between attitudes and beliefs on the one hand and practices and institutions on the other. But I would insist that certain kinds of ideas and beliefs must be present, at some level of consciousness, in the minds of the practitioners of racism. If not, we would have no way to distinguish racism from classism, ethnocentrism, sexism, religious intolerance, ageism, or any other mode of allotting differential advantages or prestige to categories of people that vary, or seem to vary, in some important respect.

A further conceptual refinement can be derived from Kwame Anthony Appiah's distinction between racism and "racialism." He defines racialism as the belief "that there are heritable characteristics, possessed by members of our species, that allow us to divide them into a small set of races, in such a way that all the members of these races share certain traits and tendencies with each other that they do not share with members of any other race."[3] Such a belief essentializes differences but does not necessarily imply inequality or hierarchy. As a moral philosopher, Appiah finds such a viewpoint mistaken but not immoral. Racialists do not become racists until they make such convictions the basis for claiming special privileges for members of what they consider to be their own race, and for disparaging and doing harm to those deemed racially Other. In an early work on color-coded racism in the United States, I implicitly made a similar distinction when I coined the phrase "romantic racialism" to describe the belief commonly held by antebellum abolitionists of both races that blacks were intrinsically different from whites in temperament and psychology (more "spiritual" and less aggressive). I did not wish to use the pejorative "racism," because, for at least some of these antislavery men and women, the alleged peculiarities of blacks did not sanction a belief in their inferiority or justify enslaving them or discriminating against them.[4] But when groups whose differing ancestry is culturally and/or physically marked come into adversarial contact, there is a powerful temptation, especially on the part of the more powerful group, to justify aggression, domination, or extermination by invoking differences defined as "racial"—meaning that they are intrinsic and unchangeable.

Unlike some sociologists, I do not believe that one can regard race and ethnicity as clearly distinct and unrelated phenomena. To my way of thinking, groups designated as races could also be regarded as "ethnic" in the Weberian sense of being historical collectivities claiming descent from a common set of ancestors. Race can therefore be described as what happens when ethnicity is deemed essential or indelible and made hierarchical.[5] There are, however, cases—and African American ethnicity would be a prime example—in which ethnic identity is created by the racialization of people who would not otherwise have shared an identity. (Blacks did not think of themselves as blacks, Negroes, or even Africans when they lived in the various kingdoms and tribal communities of West Africa before the advent of the slave trade.) From this perspective, racism is the evil twin of ethnocentrism. The latter may involve racialism in Appiah's sense but can also be based on individual cultural identities that are not viewed as unchangeable. (Many premodern communities—American Indian tribes, for example—have regarded themselves as superior beings and their enemies as utterly unworthy of respect but have nevertheless readily assimilated captives and other strangers regardless of phenotype or cultural background.) The erroneous but relatively harmless doctrine of simple racialism is rarely found among members of the advantaged or dominant groups in a plural society, but *racism* is all too common. One is more likely to find tolerant or egalitarian racialism among stigmatized groups: they may embrace and reevaluate some of the differences traditionally attributed to them, attempting to change them from defects into virtues, thus affirming a positive cultural identity and making the case that difference does not mean inferiority.

The reason that my efforts to dispense with the problematic term "racism" in some of my earlier work came to naught was simply because I could not find a satisfactory alternative to describe the phenomena that I wished to study. "White supremacy" is limited in its application to only one type of racism—what I would now call the "color-coded" or somatic variety. A review of the historical discourse on racism that began in the 1920s reveals that the term was first applied to ideologies making invidious distinctions among divisions of the "white" or Caucasian race, and especially to show that Aryans or Nordics were superior to other people normally considered "white" or "Caucasian." The term "race" has a long history, but "racism" goes back only to the early twentieth century, and the "ism" reflected the understanding of historians and others who wrote about it that they were dealing with a questionable set of beliefs and not undeniable facts of nature. It might be said that the concept of racism emerges only when the concept of race, or at least some of its applications, begin to be questioned. Our understanding of the core function of racism—its assigning of fixed or permanent differences among human descent groups and using this attribution of difference to justify their differential treatment—has changed less during the past century than have the specific categories of people who are viewed as its victims.

The historiographies of the two most conspicuous manifestations of racism—white supremacism and antisemitism—have proceeded along different tracks. Historians and sociologists concerned with one kind of racism have generally shown little interest in the work done on the other. When racism has been a central concept in this work, it has often been defined in such a group-specific way that a wider application is made difficult, if not foreclosed entirely. For example, one can readily agree with the British sociologist Zygmunt Bauman's short definition of racism, which precedes his discussion of how it applies to the Holocaust: "Man is before he acts; nothing he does may change what he is. This is roughly the philosophical essence of racism." But he then proceeds to limit the concept to cases where the aim is the extermination or expatriation of the racialized other.[6] Hence white supremacy, which normally involves the domination rather than elimination of the Other, ceases to be racism. When I myself defined the essence of racism as the ideas, practices, and institutions associated with a rigid form of ethnic hierarchy, I was unwittingly privileging the white supremacist variant over the antisemitic form, which presses toward the dissolution of the hierarchy through the expulsion or destruction of the lower-status group.[7]

Although the historiographies of white supremacy and antisemitism have not, for the most part, engaged each other, a small number of scholars, going back to the 1920s, have examined racism historically in a way that was not group-specific—as a mode of thought or set of attitudes with varying or multiple targets. Understanding which groups were considered the primary victims and how the racists whose ideas were being analyzed identified themselves and the group to which they belonged may provide a kind of lineage for my short history. But there is one aspect of these studies that may trouble some advocates of scholarly objectivity. Scholars who were hostile to what they were writing about have produced virtually all such examinations of racism. In many cases (especially at times when racism was respectable) a central purpose of their work was to discredit the ideas they were describing. While this did not mean that they were producing propaganda rather than scholarship, it did mean that they either argued for, or clearly assumed, the falsity and perniciousness of the beliefs or attitudes they were examining. But is an objective or nonjudgmental history of racism really possible? The history of racism or (as some would have it) "racisms" began as a branch of intellectual history, or the history of ideas, at a time when concepts of racial hierarchy were widely accepted. If the historian had simply described the ideas in the terms that their proponents would have found acceptable and given no direct or implicit indication that they were false and harmful, he or she would in fact have been encouraging their promulgation and contributing to their legitimization. The most fruitful orientation at a time like our own, when racism is generally condemned in principle, is a clinical one. It is legitimate to assume, at the beginning of the twenty-first century—as it might not have been at the beginning of the twentieth—that racism is an evil analogous to a deadly disease. But the responsibility of the historian or sociologist who studies racism is not to moralize and condemn but to understand this malignancy so that it can be more effectively treated, just as a medical researcher studying cancer does not moralize about it but searches for knowledge that might point the way to a cure.

The pioneer historian of racism was Théophile Simar, librarian of the Belgian colonial ministry in the 1920s. His history of what he called "la doctrine des races" was published in Brussels in 1922.[8] His provocation may have been "the rape of Belgium" by the Germans in World War I: he focused most of his critical attention on the doctrine of Germanic or Teutonic superiority over other Europeans, especially "Latin peoples," which he traced back to the pan-Germanism of the sixteenth century and to the eighteenth-century French theory that class differences could be attributed to "racial" origins. (The aristocracy was allegedly descended from the Germanic Franks and the "Third Estate" from the Gauls.) Simar was ahead of his time in maintaining that the concept of race, thus employed, lacked all scientific validity and was devised for political purposes. Most often, he contended, claims of racial superiority were a pretext for an assertion of class interests. But he rarely refers to white supremacist ideas. He includes "les blancs tout court" among the self-identifications of the master race promulgated by nineteenth century German thinkers and condemns the slaveholders of the Old South for believing that blacks belonged to a different species than whites, but nothing he wrote suggested that racism was involved in the atrocities against Africans recently committed by Belgians in the Congo. He reveals another limitation of his vision when he criticizes Houston Stewart Chamberlain for his beliefs in Germanic superiority without mentioning Chamberlain's principal obsession—antisemitism. When he gets around to discussing racist attitudes toward Jews, he dismisses antisemitic beliefs in a vast Jewish conspiracy as exaggerated and even "bizarre," but blames Jews themselves, because of their traditionalism and exclusiveness, for much of the feeling against them. Although Simar apparently employed for the first time in a historical work the terms "raciste" and "racisme," what he found most threatening about such views was their employment by Germans against other Europeans of Christian heritage.[9]

In a somewhat similar vein was Frank H. Hankins's *The Racial Basis of Civilization*, published in 1926, the first work by an American that dealt in part with the history of what the author called "racialism." It was an attack on the theory of Nordic superiority that was popularized in the United States by the writings of Madison Grant and the successful campaign for the restriction of immigration from southern and eastern Europe.[10] A sociologist who taught at Smith College, Hankins was himself a racialist in Appiah's sense (if not his own) and would today be considered a racist in his attitude toward blacks, although for him a belief in black genetic inferiority did not constitute racism or "racialism" but was simply established scientific fact. "While we are denying the extravagant claims of the Nordicists," he wrote, "we also deny the equally perverse and doctrinaire claim of the race egalitarians. There is no respect apparently in which the races are equal; but their differences must be thought of in terms of relative frequencies and not as absolute differences in kind."[11] Hankins described and sharply criticized the views of the classic European exponents of Nordicism, Teutonism, or Aryanism. "The most obvious error of the *racialists*," he concluded, "has been the claim of a purity of blood and of a specific civilizing potency which the facts do not bear out." During the recent world war, "the doctrines of race purity and superiority had a perceptibly larger significance in Germany than elsewhere."[12] Like Simar, therefore, Hankins was striking back at claims of Nordic or Teutonic supremacy that he associated with the German aggressiveness that had allegedly caused World War I. But as an American, Hankins could scarcely avoid thinking of race as also being color-coded, and here he accepted the judgments of most of his white fellow citizens. "Although the negro [*sic*] has on many occasions lived in contact with centers of advanced culture or even in the midst of them," he wrote, "he has generally lagged behind the level of such cultures." Negro backwardness is the product of biological factors, especially brain size, and therefore cannot be "explained by lack of opportunity."[13]

Hankins, the professed critic of European "racialism," thus stood on the enduring bedrock of American racism— the belief that Americans of European or white ancestry are collectively superior in intelligence and creativity to people of African descent. His single heresy, from this white supremacist perspective, was his general approval of race mixture, including intermarriage between blacks and whites. Mulattoes, he thought, had a good chance to adapt to "advanced culture," and if they were light enough to pass for white, so much the better. His biological racism was therefore more logical (some would say more Brazilian) in its application than the conventional American "one-drop rule."[14] In his references to Jews, Hankins showed little or no awareness of the dangers of a politicized antisemitism, although he did heap ridicule on some myths about Jews, such as Houston Chamberlain's fantasy that Jesus was really an Aryan. Denying that Jews were "a race in any strict sense," he described them as "a social group which in many times and places has been more vigorously hated than the negro [sic] in many parts of the United States during the last half century. The Jew has not only fought his own battle but he has 'come back' with almost obnoxious persistency and 'nerve' after every rebuff."[15] Hankins thus managed to put down blacks for their failure to rebound as Jews did, while at the same time, in his use of the adjective "obnoxious," revealing a touch of the genteel Anglo-American antisemitism that was rife in the 1920s.

With the rise of Hitler to power in Germany in 1933, the centrality of antisemitism to "the doctrine of races" or "racialism" in the modern world became fully apparent for the first time. It was Magnus Hirschfeld, prominent German sexologist of the Weimar era and early champion of homosexual rights, who first gave real currency to the term "racism" by making it the title of a book. Hirschfeld, an assimilated Jew, had the good sense to flee when the Nazis took power, and he finished his critique of Nazi ethnological theories as an exile in Nice, where he died in 1935, leaving the work unpublished. The manuscript entitled "Rassismus" was subsequently translated into English and published as *Racism* in 1938.[16] As might be expected, the book is primarily a history, analysis, and refutation of the racial doctrines that the Nazis brought with them and put into practice when they gained control of Germany. As a scientist who was ahead of his time, Hirschfeld had found little of value or substance in the concept of race: "If it were practicable, we should certainly do well to eradicate the term 'race' as far as subdivisions of the human species are concerned."[17] Hirschfeld, who thought of himself as an objective scholar and a cosmopolitan rather than an ethnic loyalist, could make analogies between Germans and Jews, which, in light of the Holocaust, would now seem offensive. "Both peoples regard themselves as elect or chosen, and both are very strongly disliked by everyone else."[18] But he perceptively described the psychosocial sources of racism when he explained the ascendancy of German antisemitism as a reaction to the loss of the First World War and the difficulties that followed. Racism, he wrote, serves as a safety valve against a sense of catastrophe. It seems "to provide for a restoration of self-esteem, for satisfaction for the assertive impulse of a will to power by tyrannizing over an enemy within the gates who was certainly more accessible and less dangerous to tackle than a reputed enemy across the national frontiers."[19]

Hirschfeld's posthumous work attracted relatively little attention. More widely noticed were the first efforts of a historian based at a major American university to address the subject of racism. French-born but American-educated, Jacques Barzun of Columbia began his very long and distinguished career as a cultural historian by studying European ideas about race. His first book, *The French Race* (1932), took up the theories and disputes among the French about the racial origins of their population. It was especially critical of efforts going back to the seventeenth century to establish the Germanic roots of the upper classes.[20] His second and more ambitious book, *Race: A Study in Modern Superstition*, originally published in 1937, was written with the urgency aroused by Hitler's coming to power in Germany.[21] In the preface Barzun's didactic purpose was made clear: "[T]he particular end or object of the work is to show how equally ill-founded are the commonplace and the learned views of race."[22] Using the adjective "racist" (which was still relatively rare) to describe the ideas of Arthur de Gobineau, Houston Chamberlain, and others whose views he was dissecting, he noted in the first chapter that racism was not unique to German attitudes toward Jews but could be found in the widespread assumption that "the whites are unquestionably superior to the colored races," in the fears of a "yellow peril" from Asia, and in the belief that "the great American problem is to keep the Anglo-Saxon race pure from the contamination of Negro (or Southern European or Jewish) 'blood.'" In a misguided attempt at evenhandedness (similar to that of Hirschfeld), he opined that "[t]he Semite himself is race conscious and given his chance, just as scornful and prejudiced as the Aryan who would oppress him."[23] Barzun conveyed how broadly he conceived of his subject when he broke European racism of the late nineteenth century into four distinct tendencies: (1) racializing the rivalry between Germany and France as Aryanism versus Celtism; (2) attributing the rise of socialism to a Jewish conspiracy; (3) asserting that the German races are rising and that the Latin races are declining; and (4) believing that civilized whites must unify to hold in check "the colored hordes of black, red, and yellow men whom they have aroused from their ancestral torpor, else European culture—or rather civilization itself—is doomed." He concluded: "No European figure of any importance in any walk of life escaped, during that period [1870–1900], the contamination of one or more of these beliefs."[24]

Despite being aware of the full scale of his subject, Barzun concentrated almost all of his attention as a historian of ideas on those thinkers who laid the foundation for the Nazi embrace of Aryanism. Yet the specifically antisemitic application of Aryanism receives surprisingly little attention. "Race in Germany," he explained, "was a means to give back to the German people a feeling of self-respect after the national humiliation at Versailles and since." He then went on to describe similar uses of racism for the purpose of "national uplift" in other times and places.[25] No mention was made of the Nuremberg Laws of 1935, which made racism official policy to a degree unparalleled in world history (although they were nearly approximated in some of the southern states of the United States), and the book's treatment of German antisemitism gives the reader little reason to anticipate the full horror of what would soon be happening to Jews in Germany. Despite the time-bound limitations of its vision, Barzun's *Race* did set two important precedents for most future historians of racism: it presumed that the claims of the innate inferiority of one "race" to another were false or at least unproven, and its main concern was with the history of ideas rather than with the social and political applications of prejudiced beliefs and attitudes.

The outbreak of World War II brought German racial ideology into sharper focus as the pernicious ideas of an evil enemy. Even before the United States had entered the war, the prominent cultural anthropologist Ruth Benedict gave the term "racism" popular currency in her book *Race: Science and Politics*, originally published in 1940 but reissued several times thereafter. The first chapter was entitled "Racism: The *ism* of the Modern World," and another, called "A Natural History of Racism," established some of the central themes of later and more detailed histories of the subject. Her main concern was to refute the scientific pretensions of believers in racial inequality, but she also provided both a historical account and a theoretical discussion of the relation between racial and religious intolerance. When she was functioning as a historian of ideas, she distinguished sharply between religious and racial conceptions of difference. After apparently limiting the concept of racism to theories based on natural science that did not come to prominence before the nineteenth century, she went on to probe the psychology of "race prejudice" and attempted to establish a functional equivalency between religious bigotry and animosities ostensibly based on physical type or ancestry. She viewed them both as leading to forms of "persecution" that differed only in how they were rationalized, and not in their essential nature. "Racism remains, in the eyes of history," she maintained, ". . . merely another instance of the persecution of minorities for the advantage of those in power." From this perspective, "the Third Reich is but following a long series of precedents in European anti-Semitism."[26] She attributed American prejudice against blacks to "the persistence of slave-owner attitudes." But she exposed the limits of racial liberalism in the United States in 1940 when she called for a better deal for African Americans while conspicuously failing to advocate full and immediate equality: "Granted that great numbers of Negroes are not ready for full citizenship, the social conditions which perpetuate their poverty and ignorance must be remedied before anyone can judge what kind of citizens they might be in other, more favorable circumstances."[27]

The war and the Holocaust inspired a vast outpouring of literature on the history of antisemitism, much of it stressing its religious roots and eschewing comparisons with racism targeted at other groups. Disagreements developed on the question of whether the Nazi urge to eliminate Jews on the basis of "race hygiene" was a continuation of earlier antisemitic attitudes based, ostensibly at least, on religion, or whether it was a radical new departure, a sine qua non for the Holocaust.[28] Those who endorsed the latter view sometimes employed a definition of racism that would make the term apply only to "eliminationist antisemitism."

Meanwhile many critical social-scientific studies of prejudice and discrimination against blacks followed in the wake of Gunnar Myrdal's *An American Dilemma* of 1944. This epoch-making work brought to broad public notice for the first time the fact that the foundation-supported social science community, spurred by revulsion against racism inspired by Hitler's policies, had reached a consensus that Jim Crow segregation was unjustified and indeed un-American.[29] The favored term in early works criticizing white supremacy in the United States was "race prejudice" rather than "racism." Not until the 1960s did the latter term come into general use to describe attitudes toward African Americans, and then it was at first limited to the intellectual content of the beliefs and not to the behavior with which it was associated. But as popular usage of the term came to encompass prejudice and discrimination as well as doctrine, many historians concerned with black-white relations in the United States began to use the term casually, without reflecting much on its meaning. At its most imprecise, it could mean anything that whites did or thought that worked to the disadvantage of blacks. In the 1960s and 1970s intellectual and social historians produced a number of major works on color-coded racism or white supremacy as theory, belief system, or ideology. This work was inspired, not only by the civil rights movement in the United States, but also by the decolonization of Africa and a growing awareness that there were race questions in the other former slave societies of the Americas.[30]

Since the bifurcation of studies of white supremacy and antisemitism that took place after World War II, there have been few serious efforts to write histories of racism that encompass both the antisemitic and the color-coded varieties. The first comprehensive history of American racism, Thomas Gossett's *Race: The History of an Idea in America* (1963) traced consciousness of race to the ancient world.[31] Its treatment of specifically American manifestations cast its net quite wide to include representation and treatment of American Indians and immigrants from southern and eastern Europe, including Jews, as well as blacks. But most subsequent work on the history of American racism has been group-specific and has concentrated most heavily on attitudes toward African Americans. On the other hand, George Mosse's general history of European racism, published in 1978, focused mainly on the growth of racist antisemitism and paid relatively little attention to the color-coded racism associated with imperial expansion.[32] There appear to be only two significant attempts to cover Western attitudes toward race comprehensively: Ivan Hannaford's *Race: The History of an Idea in the West* (1996)[33] and Imanuel Geiss, *Geschichte der Rassismus* (History of racism) published in Germany in 1988 and never translated into English.[34] Hannaford's study, as its title indicates, is strictly an intellectual history and considers race as a concept more than racism as an ideology. It argues strenuously that no clear concept of race existed before the seventeenth century, thus raising the issue of whether anything that existed before the invention of race in the modern sense can legitimately be labeled racism. Geiss, to the contrary, sees racism as anticipated in most respects by the ethnocentrism or xenophobia that developed in the ancient world, as reflected, for example, in the Old Testament.

My own conception, as set forth in the introduction and applied throughout the *Short History,* falls between Hannaford's view that race and racism are peculiarly modern ideas and Geiss's notion that they are simply manifestations of the perennial phenomena of ethnocentrism and xenophobia. I have attempted to develop an understanding that is neither too broad for historical specificity nor too narrow to cover more than the limited span of Western history during which a racism based on scientific theories of human variation was widely accepted. If racism is defined as an ideology rather than as a theory, links can be established between belief and practice that the history of ideas may obscure. But ideologies have content, and it is necessary to distinguish racist ideologies from other belief systems that emphasize human differences and can be used as rationalizations of inequality. The classic sociological distinction between racism and ethnocentrism is helpful, but not perhaps in the usual sense, in which the key variable is whether differences are described in cultural or physical terms. It is actually quite difficult in specific historical cases to say whether appearance or "culture" is the source of the salient differences, because culture can be reified and essentialized to the point where it has the same deterministic effect as skin color. But we would be stretching the concept of racism much too far if we attempted to make it cover the pride and loyalty that may result from a strong sense of ethnic identity. Such group-centeredness may engender prejudice and discrimination against those outside the group, but two additional elements would seem to be required before the categorization of racism is justified.

One is a belief that the differences between the ethnic groups involved are permanent and ineradicable. If conversion or assimilation is a real possibility, we have religious or cultural intolerance but not racism. The second is the social and political side of the ideology—its linkage to the exercise of power in the name of race and the resulting patterns of domination or exclusion. To attempt a short formulation, we might say that racism exists when one ethnic group or historical collectivity dominates, excludes, or seeks to eliminate another on the basis of differences that it believes are hereditary and unalterable.

N O T E S

INTRODUCTION

1. See, for example, George Reid Andrews, *Blacks and Whites in São Paulo, Brazil, 1888–1988* (Madison, 1991); and France Winddance Twine, *Racism in a Racial Democracy: The Maintenance of White Supremacy in Brazil* (New Brunswick, N.J., 1998).

2. For a fuller discussion of the concept of racism in historical discourse and historiography, see the appendix to this volume.

3. See Uli Linke, *Blood and Nation: The European Aesthetics of Race* (Philadelphia, 1999).

4. John Solomos and Les Back, *Racism and Society* (Houndsmills, Basingstoke, 1996), 18–19, 213.

5. Pierre-André Taguieff, *La force du préjugé: Essai sur le racisme et ses doubles* (Paris, 1987), 62–63.

6. Joel Kovel, *White Racism: A Psychohistory* (New York, 1970), 31–32 and passim. For some nineteenth-century expressions of the exclusionary or aversive attitude toward the black presence, see George M. Fredrickson, *The Black Image in the White Mind: The Debate on Afro-American Character and Destiny, 1817–1914* (Middletown, Conn., 1987; orig. pub. 1971), 130–164, 228–255, and passim.

7. See Kosaku Yoshino, "The Discourse on Blood and Racial Identity in Contemporary Japan," in *The Construction of Racial Identity in China and Japan: Historical and Contemporary Perspectives*, ed. Frank Dikötter (London, 1997), 199–211.

8. See Philip Mason, *Patterns of Dominance* (London, 1970), 13–20.

O N E   *Religion and the Invention of Racism*

1. Ivan Hannaford, *Race: The History of an Idea in the West* (Baltimore, 1996), 17–57.

2. Lloyd A. Thompson, *Romans and Blacks* (London, 1989).

3. Frank M. Snowden, Jr., *Before Color Prejudice: The Ancient View of Blacks* (Cambridge, Mass., 1983), 101–107 and passim. See also Snowden's *Blacks in Antiquity: Ethiopians in the Greco-Roman Experience* (Cambridge, Mass, 1970).

4. Léon Poliakov, *The History of Anti-Semitism*, vol. I, *From the Time of Christ to the Court Jews*, trans. Richard Howard (New York, 1965), 21.

5. For somewhat differing views of the transformation from anti-Judaism to antisemitism, see Gavin I. Langmuir, *Toward a Definition of Antisemitism* (Berkeley, 1990), 63–133; and Robert Chazan, *Medieval Stereotypes and Modern Antisemitism* (Berkeley, 1997), 129–138.

6. On the power of conversion, see Gavin I. Langmuir, *History, Religion and Antisemitism* (Berkeley, 1990), 292; and Norman Cohn, *The Pursuit of the Millennium: Revolutionary Millenarians and Mystical Anarchists of the Middle Ages* (New York, 1970), 70, 80. See Mark R. Cohen, *Under Crescent and Cross: The Jews in the Middle Ages* (Princeton, 1994), 77–88, for a succinct account of the changing economic role of medieval Jewry.

7. Langmuir, *Toward a Definition*, 209–281. See also Miri Rubin, *Gentile Tales: The Narrative Assault on Medieval Jews* (New Haven, 1999).

8. Poliakov, *History of Anti-Semitism*, 1:137–144.

9. Quoted in Cohen, *Under Crescent and Cross*, 172.

10. Joshua Trachtenberg, *The Devil and the Jews: The Medieval Conception of the Jew and Its Relation to Modern Antisemitism* (Philadelphia, 1983; orig. pub. 1943), 18.

11. See the forward by Marc Saperstein to the 1983 edition of *The Devil and the Jews*.

12. Miraculous tales in which the direct intercession of the Virgin dissolved the pact that a repentant sinner had previously made with Satan suggest that no one was considered totally beyond redemption by medieval Christians, but such rare exceptions tended to prove the rule of Jewish irredeemability more than they contradicted it.

13. This point will be addressed more fully in the comparison of modern antisemitism and white supremacy in chap. 2.

14. Langmuir, *Toward a Definition*, 100–133; Chazan, *Medieval Stereotypes*, 90–91.

15. Robert Bartlett, *The Making of Europe: Conquest, Colonization, and Cultural Change, 950–1350* (Princeton, 1993), 239–240 and passim.

16. Ibid., 237–239.

17. R. I. Moore, *The Formation of a Persecuting Society: Power and Deviance in Western Europe, 950–1250* (Oxford, 1987).

18. Winthrop D. Jordan, *White over Black: American Attitudes toward the Negro, 1550–1812* (Chapel Hill, 1968), 4–11; Jean Devisse, *The Image of the Black in Western Art*, vol. 2, *From the Early Christian Era to the "Age of Discovery,"* pt. 1, *From the Demonic Threat to the Incarnation of Sainthood* (New York, 1979), passim.

19. Henri Baudet, *Paradise on Earth: Some Thoughts on European Images of Non-European Man*, trans. Elizabeth Wentholt (New Haven, 1965).

20. John Block Friedman, *The Monstrous Races in Medieval Art and Thought* (Cambridge, Mass., 1981), 59–60, 64–65. See also Snowden, *Before Color Prejudice*, 101–107.

21. Jean Devisse and Michel Mollat, *The Image of the Black in Western Art*, vol. 2, pt. 2, *Africans in the Christian Ordinance of the World, Fourteenth to Sixteenth Century* (New York, 1979), 24–30, 90–128; Jan Nederveen Pieterse, *White on Black: Images of Africa and Blacks in Western Popular Culture* (New Haven, 1992), 24–25.

22. Devisse, *Black in Western Art*, vol. 2, pt. 1, 138, 158–205; William Chester Jordan, "The Medieval Background," in *Struggles in the Promised Land: Toward a History of Black-Jewish Relations in the United States*, ed. Jack Salzman and Cornel West (New York,

1997), 57. I disagree, however, with Jordan's conclusion that such positive images were outweighed by negative ones. I draw a different conclusion from the work of Devisse, Pieterse, and others.

23. James H. Sweet, "The Iberian Roots of American Racist Thought," *William and Mary Quarterly* 54 (1997): 143–166.

24. Bernard Lewis, *Race and Slavery in the Middle East* (New York, 1990), 44–45, 55; William McKee Evans, "From the Land of Canaan to the Land of Guinea," *American Historical Review* 85 (1980): 15–43.

25. Bernard Lewis, *Race and Color in Islam* (New York, 1971), 38, 64–65; Sweet, "Iberian Roots," 157–164.

26. John Thornton, *Africa and Africans in the Making of the Atlantic World, 1400–1800,* 2d ed. (Cambridge, Eng., 1992), 72–97.

27. Michael Adas, *Machines as the Measure of Men: Science, Technology, and Ideologies of Western Dominance* (Ithaca, 1989), 65–68, and Thornton, *Africa and Africans,* 143–148.

28. Léon Poliakov, *The History of Anti-Semitism,* vol. 2, *From Mohammed to the Marranos,* trans. Natalie Gerardi (New York, 1973), 116–145.

29. In an effort to induce *conversos* to return to the fold, Sephardic Jewish writers later promulgated the doctrine that such forced conversions did not represent true apostasy from Judaism and were thus forgivable.

30. The fullest account of these developments is B. Netanyahu, *The Origins of the Inquisition in Fifteenth Century Spain* (New York, 1995). I gained insight into what the sheer numbers meant from communications with Benjamin Braude.

31. A useful account of how the Inquisition dealt with those of Jewish descent after the fifteenth century can be found in Henry Kamen, *The Spanish Inquisition: An Historical Revision* (London, 1997).

32. Netanyahu, *Origins,* 314–327; Kamen, *Inquisition,* 236–238 and passim.

33. Poliakov, *History of Anti-Semitism,* 2:181–182.

34. Netanyahu, *Origins,* 1052–1054; Kamen, *Inquisition,* 230–254; Poliakov, *History of Anti-Semitism,* 2:170–232, 279–301. See also

Yosef Hayim Yerushalmi, *Assimilation and Racial Anti-Semitism: The Iberian and German Models*, Leo Baeck Memorial Lecture 26 (New York, 1982).

35. Bartlett, *Making of Europe*, 240–242; Poliakov, *History of Anti-Semitism*, 2:328–357.

36. See Friedman, *Monstrous Races*.

37. Eduardo Aznar Vallejo, "The Conquests of the Canary Islands," in *Implicit Understandings: Observing, Reporting, and Reflecting on the Encounters between Europeans and Other Peoples in the Early Modern Era*, ed. Stuart B. Schwartz (Cambridge, Eng., 1994), 134–156.

38. Ronald Sanders, *Lost Tribes and Promised Lands: The Origins of American Racism* (Boston, 1978), 92–102.

39. Quoted in Anthony Pagden, *The Fall of Natural Man: The American Indian and the Origins of Comparative Ethnology* (Cambridge, Eng., 1982), 116.

40. Quoted in ibid., 140. See 109–144 for a good account of the debate.

41. For a more detailed account of the debate between Las Casas and Sepúlveda, see Lewis Hanke, *Aristotle and the American Indians* (Bloomington, Ind., 1970; orig. pub. 1959). Las Casas later came to regret his endorsement of African enslavement.

42. Pagden, *Fall of Natural Man*, 33, 38.

43. Sanders, *Lost Tribes*, 114, 120–121, 343–344; Robin Blackburn, *The Making of New World Slavery: From the Baroque to the Modern, 1492–1800* (London, 1997), 64–76; Jordan, *White over Black*, 15–19.

44. Magnus Mörner, *Race Mixture in the History of Latin America* (Boston, 1967). See also Carl Degler, *Neither Black nor White: Slavery and Race Relations in Brazil and the United States* (New York, 1971).

45. This paragraph is indebted to an excellent piece of unpublished scholarship—Noam Leslau, "A Conflict of Nations: *Limpieza de Sangre*, Medieval Communities, and the Emergence of Spanish National Identity" (honors thesis in history, Stanford University, 1999).

46. The analogy to the Nazis is made by Netanyahu in *Origins* and by Yerushalmi in *Assimilation and Racial Anti-Semitism.* Both, however, give some weight to the difference between religiously based and secular constructions of innate Jewish difference.

47. Poliakov, *History of Anti-Semitism,* 2:230–231.

48. Quoted in Mörner, *Race Mixture,* 55–56.

49. See Thornton, *Africa and Africans,* 269–271.

50. See George M. Fredrickson, *White Supremacy: A Comparative Study in American and South African History* (New York, 1981), 73.

51. See references in nn. 24 and 43 above.

52. On the confusion surrounding the Curse of Ham in the late medieval and early modern periods, see Benjamin Braude, "The Sons of Noah and the Construction of Ethnic and Geographical Identities in the Medieval and Early Modern Periods," *William and Mary Quarterly* 54 (1997): 103–142. On the uses of the curse to justify radical status inequality within Europe, see Paul Freedman, *Images of the Medieval Peasant* (Stanford, 1999), 86–104.

53. Sanders, *Lost Tribes,* 62.

54. Benjamin Braude, "Race and Sex: What Happened to Cross-Color Generation in the Eighteenth Century?" (paper presented to the Conference on Sexuality in Early America, Philadelphia, June 1–3, 2001), 17–18.

55. See Thomas Virgil Peterson, *Ham and Japheth: The Mythic World of Whites in the Antebellum South* (Metuchen, N.J., 1978). Blackburn, in *New World Slavery* (72–73), criticizes David Brion Davis for contending that the Curse of Ham had little importance as a justification of slavery before the late eighteenth and nineteenth centuries (*Slavery and Human Progress* [New York, 1984], 337 n. 144). In my view the curse was not securely linked to the polemical defense of slavery until it became an alternative rationale for southerners who resisted scientific racism on fundamentalist religious grounds.

56. I have described this transition elsewhere. See "Social Origins of American Racism," in *The Arrogance of Race: Historical Per-*

spectives on Slavery, Racism, and Social Inequality (Middletown, Conn., 1988), 189–205; and *White Supremacy*, 76–80. On seventeenth-century Protestant doubts and rationalizations concerning slavery, see David Brion Davis, *The Problem of Slavery in Western Culture* (Ithaca, 1966), 165–222, passim.

T W O *The Rise of Modern Racism(s)*

1. Léon Poliakov, *The Aryan Myth: A History of Racist and Nationalist Ideas in Europe*, trans. Edmund Howard (New York, 1996; orig. pub. 1971), 130–144.

2. See Audrey Smedley, *Race in North America: Origin and Evolution of a Worldview* (Boulder, 1993), 36–40, for a good account of early use of the word "race." The citation from the Spanish dictionary is quoted on 38–39. On the mythic meanings attached to blood and its transmission, see Uli Linke, *Blood and Nation: The European Aesthetics of Race* (Philadelphia, 1999).

3. Winthrop D. Jordan, *White over Black: American Attitudes toward the Negro, 1550–1812* (Chapel Hill, 1968), 97.

4. John Thornton, *Africa and Africans in the Making of the Atlantic World, 1400–1800*, 2d ed. (Cambridge, Eng., 1992), 146–148; George M. Fredrickson, *White Supremacy: A Comparative Study in American and South African History* (New York, 1981), 76–80. See also T. H. Breen and Stephen Innes, *"Myne Owne Ground": Race and Freedom on Virginia's Eastern Shore, 1640–1676* (New York, 1980).

5. J. Jean Hecht, *Continental and Colonial Servants in Eighteenth Century England* (Northampton, Mass., 1954), 56; William B. Cohen, *The French Encounter with Africans: White Response to Blacks, 1530–1880* (Bloomington, Ind., 1980), 112–113: Sue Peabody, *"There Are No Slaves in France": The Political Culture of Race and Slavery in the Ancien Régime* (New York, 1996), 116–130.

6. David Sorkin, *The Transformation of German Jewry, 1780–1840* (New York, 1987), 43; Jacob Katz, *Out of the Ghetto: The Social Background of Jewish Emancipation, 1770–1870* (Cambridge, Mass., 1973), 28–29.

7. Peter Pulzer, *Jews and the German State: The Political History of a Minority* (Oxford, 1992), 69.

8. Emmanuel Chukwudi Eze, ed., *Race and the Enlightenment: A Reader* (Cambridge, Mass., 1997), 13. Another useful anthology of racial thought in the formative era of scientific racism is H. F. Augstein, ed., *Race: The Origins of an Idea, 1760–1850* (Bristol, 1996). Eze focuses on Continental thought and Augstein mostly on British.

9. Eze, *Race and the Enlightenment*, 83–87; see also Augstein, *Race*, 58–67.

10. For an extended discussion of the chain of being and its application to race in the eighteenth century, see Jordan, *White over Black*, 216–239.

11. Eze, *Race and the Enlightenment*, 15–28; Augstein, *Race*, 1–9.

12. Quoted in Peabody, *"There Are No Slaves,"* 66.

13. See Jordan, *White over Black*, 512–525 and passim.

14. Quoted in Michael Burleigh and Wolfgang Wipperman, *The Racial State: Germany, 1933–1945* (Cambridge, Eng., 1991), 24.

15. Thomas Jefferson, *Notes on Virginia* (1784), in *The Life and Selected Writings of Thomas Jefferson*, ed. Adrienne Koch and William Peden (New York, 1944), 256–262.

16. Quoted in Poliakov, *Aryan Myth*, 158–159.

17. See H. Hoetink, *The Two Variants of Caribbean Race Relations: A Contribution to the Sociology of Segmented Societies*, trans. Eva M. Hooykaas (London, 1967).

18. Alden T. Vaughan, *Roots of American Racism: Essays on the Colonial Experience* (New York, 1995), 16–19, 33.

19. George M. Fredrickson, *White Supremacy: A Comparative Study in American and South African History* (New York, 1981), 39–40, 116–117.

20. Lionel B. Steiman, *Paths to Genocide: Antisemitism in Western History* (New York, 1998), 137.

21. Michael Adas, *Machines as the Measure of Men: Science, Technology, and Ideologies of Western Dominance* (Ithaca, 1989), 291 and passim.

22. See Arthur Hertzberg, *The French Enlightenment and the Jews* (New York, 1968), 280–313; Cohen, *The French Encounter*, 84–85; and Pierre Pluchon, *Nègres et juifs au XVIIIe siècle: Le racisme au siècle des lumières* (Paris, 1984), 69–71.

23. On Voltaire's views on slavery, which were not entirely consistent, see David Brion Davis, *The Problem of Slavery in Western Culture* (Ithaca, 1966), 392n, 401–402. The plight of black slaves is, of course, portrayed sympathetically in *Candide*. My own view of Voltaire has been influenced by Peter Gay, *The Enlightenment: The Rise of Modern Paganism* (New York, 1966), and by Gay's essay, "Voltaire's Anti-Semitism," in *The Party of Humanity: Essays in the French Enlightenment* (New York, 1964), 97–108.

24. Anthony J. Barker, *The African Link: British Attitudes to the Negro in the Era of the Atlantic Slave Trade, 1550–1807* (London, 1978), 46–48, 163–177; Michael Banton, *Racial Theories*, 2d ed. (Cambridge, Eng., 1998), 27; Seymour Drescher, *From Slavery to Freedom: Comparative Studies in the Rise and Fall of Atlantic Slavery* (Houndsmills, Basingstoke, 1999), 285.

25. On how the British evangelical movement offered effective resistance to biological racism during the first third of the nineteenth century, see Philip D. Curtin, *The Image of Africa: British Ideas and Action, 1780–1850* (Madison, 1964), 229–243.

26. Katz, *Out of the Ghetto*, 196–197.

27. Augstein, *Race*, 86–88.

28. Drescher, *From Slavery to Freedom*, 291–300.

29. See George M. Fredrickson, *The Black Image in the White Mind: The Debate on Afro-American Character and Destiny, 1817–1914* (Middletown, Conn., 1987; orig. pub. 1971), chap. 3; and William R. Stanton, *The Leopard's Spots: Scientific Attitudes toward Race in America, 1815–1859* (Chicago, 1960).

30. Quoted in Drescher, *From Slavery to Freedom*, 291. See also Poliakov, *Aryan Myth*, 224–230.

31. Poliakov, *Aryan Myth*, 182; Augstein, *Race*, 162–180. The American translation by J. H. Guenebault that is reprinted by Augstein has obviously been edited by the translator, as clearly re-

vealed by citations to works published well after the original French publication date.

32. Drescher, *From Slavery to Freedom*, 295–299.

33. Fredrickson, *Black Image*, 58–64, 90–96.

34. On the distinction between civic and ethnic nationalism, see Liah Greenfeld, *Nationalism: Five Roads to Modernity* (Cambridge, Mass., 1992).

35. Quoted in Jacob Katz, *From Prejudice to Destruction: Anti-Semitism, 1700–1933* (Cambridge, Mass., 1980), 60. On Herder's ideas, see Johann Gottfried Herder, *Reflections on the Philosophy of the History of Mankind*, ed. Frank E. Manuel (Chicago, 1968); Anthony Pagden, *European Encounters with the New World: From Renaissance to Romanticism* (New Haven, 1993), 172–180; and Dietz Bering, "Jews and the German Language," in *Identity and Intolerance: Nationalism, Racism, and Xenophobia in Germany and the United States*, ed. Norbert Finzsch and Dietmar Schirmer (Cambridge, Eng., 1998), 256–260.

36. Johann Gottlieb Fichte, *Beitrag zur Berichtigung der Urteile des Publikums ueber die Franzoesische Revolution* (1793), excerpted in Paul Mendes-Flohr and Jehuda Reinharz, *The Jew in the Modern World: A Documentary History* (New York, 1995), 309 (trans. by M. Gelber).

37. Pulzer, *Jews and the German State*, 43.

38. On Treitschke, see Ute Gerhard, "The Discursive Construction of National Stereotypes," in Finzsch and Schirmer, *Identity and Intolerance*, 85–88; and George L. Mosse, *Toward the Final Solution: A History of European Racism* (Madison, 1985; orig. pub. 1978), 148.

39. See Frederick E. Hoxie, *A Final Promise: The Campaign to Assimilate the Indians, 1880–1920* (Lincoln, Neb., 1984).

40. On antebellum Anglo-Saxonism, see especially Reginald Horsman, *Race and Manifest Destiny: The Origins of American Racial Anglo-Saxonism* (Cambridge, Mass., 1981).

41. See John Higham, *Strangers in the Land: Patterns of American Nativism, 1860–1925* (New Brunswick, N.J., 1955); and Matthew

Frye Jacobson, *Whiteness of a Different Color: European Immigrants and the Alchemy of Race* (Cambridge, Mass., 1998).

42. Michael Omi and Howard Winant, *Racial Formation in the United States: From the 1960s to the 1990s* (New York, 1994), 71.

43. The standard works on the Jewish experience of emancipation are Katz, *Out of the Ghetto*, and Sorkin, *Transformation of German Jewry.*

44. See Peter Pulzer, *The Rise of Political Anti-Semitism in Germany and Austria*, rev. ed. (Cambridge, Mass., 1988; orig. pub. 1964).

45. These events are described and analyzed in James F. Harris, *The People Speak! Anti-Semitism and Emancipation in Nineteenth-Century Bavaria* (Ann Arbor, 1994).

46. The unevenness of emancipation is described in Katz, *Out of the Ghetto*, and in Pulzer, *Jews and the German State.*

47. Sorkin, *Transformation of German Jewry,* 109, 173 (quotation), and passim.

48. On the impact of Marr's book, see John Weiss, *Ideology of Death: Why the Holocaust Happened in Germany* (Chicago, 1996), 97–98; and Katz, *From Prejudice to Destruction,* 260–261.

49. Mosse, *Final Solution,* 164–166; Katz, *From Prejudice to Destruction,* 265–269.

50. Fredrickson, *Black Image,* chap. 2.

51. Ibid., 76–90.

52. Thomas Virgil Peterson, *Ham and Japheth: The Mythic World of Whites in the Antebellum South* (Metuchen, N.J., 1978).

53. See George M. Fredrickson, *The Arrogance of Race: Historical Perspectives on Slavery, Racism, and Social Inequality* (Middletown, Conn., 1988), 15–27, for a discussion of efforts to reconcile race and class in antebellum South Carolina.

54. See Leon F. Litwack, *North of Slavery: The Negro in the Free States, 1790–1860* (Chicago, 1961), and Joanne Pope Melish, *Disowning Slavery: Gradual Emancipation and "Race" in New England, 1780–1860* (Ithaca, 1998).

55. Rayford W. Logan, *The Betrayal of the Negro: From Rutherford B. Hayes to Woodrow Wilson* (New York, 1965).

56. The fullest account of the changing image of blacks can be found in Joel Williamson, *The Crucible of Race: Black-White Relations in the American South since Emancipation* (New York, 1984). See also Fredrickson, *Black Image*, chap. 9.

57. See Pierre L. van den Berghe, *Race and Racism: A Comparative Perspective* (New York, 1967), on the transition, following emancipation, from "paternalist" to "competitive" race relations. Van den Berghe, however, applies his model only to color-coded societies. It applies almost as well, in my opinion, to societies where Jews rather than blacks are being "emancipated."

58. On Bismarck's change of course, see Gordon A. Craig, *Germany, 1866–1945* (New York, 1978), 144–157; and Pulzer, *Rise of Political Anti-Semitism*, 91–92.

59. My view of southern political history during this period continues to be influenced by the classic works of C. Vann Woodward, *Origins of the New South, 1877–1913* (Baton Rouge, 1951), and *The Strange Career of Jim Crow*, 3d rev. ed. (New York, 1974). But a new book by Michael Perman brings the playing of the race card by the Democrats into sharper focus. See his *Struggle for Mastery: Disfranchisement in the South, 1888–1908* (Chapel Hill, 2001).

60. Pulzer, *Rise of Political Anti-Semitism*, 83–119.

61. Craig, *Germany*, 83–85.

62. Mark Summers, *Railroads, Reconstruction, and the Gospel of Prosperity: Aid under the Radical Republicans, 1865–1877* (Princeton, 1984), 268–298; Eric Foner, *Reconstruction: America's Unfinished Revolution, 1863–1877* (New York, 1988), 512–553.

63. Foner, *Reconstruction*, 517–519.

64. Fredrickson, *Black Image*, chap. 8; George W. Stocking, Jr., *Race, Culture, and Evolution: Essays in the History of Anthropology* (New York, 1968), 112–132.

65. There is a substantial historical literature on the eugenics movements. The British side of the story is well covered in Nancy Stepan, *The Idea of Race in Science: Great Britain, 1800–1960* (Hamden, Conn., 1982). On American eugenics, an older standard account is Mark H. Haller, *Eugenics: Hereditarian Attitudes in American Thought* (New Brunswick, N.J., 1963). More recently Daniel J.

Kevles has produced a lively and updated narrative: *In the Name of Eugenics: Genetics and the Uses of Human Heredity* (Berkeley, 1986).

66. David Montgomery, *The Fall of the House of Labor: The Workplace, the State, and American Labor Activism, 1865–1925* (New York, 1987), 25, 46, 81–87, and passim. See also David R. Roediger, *The Wages of Whiteness: Race and the Making of the American Working Class* (New York, 1991).

67. W.E.B. Du Bois, *Black Reconstruction in America, 1860–1880* (New York, 1970; orig. pub. 1935), 701.

68. See Max Weber's powerful and perceptive discussion of "ethnic status" among southern poor whites in *Economy and Society*, ed. Guenther Roth and Claus Wittich, trans. Ephram Fischoff et al. (Berkeley, 1978), 385–387.

69. Weiss, *Ideology of Death*, 106.

70. The classic studies of the *völkisch* nationalism in German thought are Fritz Richard Stern, *The Politics of Cultural Despair: A Study in the Rise of the German Ideology* (Berkeley, 1961); and George Mosse, *The Crisis of German Ideology: Intellectual Origins of the Third Reich* (New York, 1964).

71. Houston Stewart Chamberlain, *Foundations of the Nineteenth Century*, 2 vols. (London, 1911).

72. This was the theme, most obviously, of Wilhelm Marr's *Der Sieg des Judentums über das Germanentum* (1873).

73. See Fredrickson, *Black Image*, chaps. 8 and 9; and Williamson, *Crucible of Race*, 111–124.

74. See Jacobson, *Whiteness of a Different Color*.

75. See Rogers M. Smith, *Civic Ideals: Conflicting Visions of Citizenship in U.S. History* (New Haven, 1997), 346–469; and Desmond King, *Making Americans: Immigration, Race, and the Origins of the Diverse Democracy* (Cambridge, Mass., 2000).

76. John Rex, *Race Relations in Sociological Theory* (London, 1970).

77. See the essays in Daniel Chirot and Anthony Reid, *Essential Outsiders: Chinese and Jews in the Modern Transformation of Southeast Asia and Central Europe* (Seattle, 1997).

78. For a theoretical understanding of this process, see Herbert Blumer's seminal essay "Race Prejudice as a Sense of Group Position," *Pacific Sociological Review* 1 (1958): 3–7.

79. See chap. 3 below for a discussion of some of these contingencies.

80. This is the enduring truth that survives from the American consensus historiography of the 1950s and from the school of historians who stress German exceptionalism or *ein Sonderweg*. The lesson should be that every nation's history is exceptional, not that one is peculiar in ways that make it stand out against some abstract model of normality or typicality.

THREE *Climax and Retreat*

1. The adjective is necessary because the word "regime" can be used to describe a prevailing system of domination the basis of which is implicit or de facto rather than explicit and de jure. I was tempted to use the concept of "the racial state," as developed by Michael Burleigh and Wolfgang Wippermann in *The Racial State: Germany, 1933–1945* (Cambridge, Eng., 1991), but their usage emphasized some features of the Nazi regime's practice of "racial hygiene" that were not replicated in South Africa or the American South. The Nazis were unique in the extent to which they tried to improve the quality of the "master race" through the elimination of its "unfit" members.

2. See John W. Cell, *The Highest Stage of White Supremacy: The Origins of Segregation in South Africa and the American South* (Cambridge, Eng., 1982). But in my view the preapartheid segregation policy in South Africa did not meet the criteria for a racist regime as fully as did the Jim Crow system in the American South. Unlike Cell, I would make a typological distinction between colonialist and racist regimes. It was not until after 1948 that South Africa completed its evolution from the former to the latter. A work that highlights the modern aspect of apartheid is Heribert Adam, *Modernizing Racial Domination: South Africa's Political Dynamics* (Berkeley, 1971).

3. Zygmunt Bauman, *Modernity and the Holocaust* (Ithaca, 1989).

4. On the ideology of the civilizing mission and how it worked against extreme or consistent racism, see Michael Adas, *Machines as the Measure of Men: Science, Technology, and Ideologies of Western Dominance* (Ithaca, 1989), especially 199–270.

5. The literature on Latin American race relations is enormous, but especially relevant to our concerns are the comparative perspectives on Brazil to be found in Anthony W. Marx, *Making Race and Nation: A Comparison of South Africa, the United States, and Brazil* (Cambridge, Eng., 1998); George Reid Andrews, *Blacks and Whites in S{{atilde}}o Paulo, Brazil, 1888–1988* (Madison, 1991); and Antonio Sérgio Alfredo Guimar{{atilde}}es, *Racismo e anti-racismo no Brasil* (S{{atilde}}o Paulo, 1999).

6. Andrews, *Blacks and Whites*, 4.

7. See Bruce F. Pauley, *From Prejudice to Persecution: A History of Austrian Anti-Semitism* (Chapel Hill, 1992), 27–60.

8. Léon Poliakov, *The History of Anti-Semitism*, vol. 4, *Suicidal Europe, 1870–1933*, trans. George Klim (New York, 1985), 127 and 67–134, passim.

9. This is a point effectively made by Cell in *Highest Stage of White Supremacy.*

10. See Peter Warwick, *Black People and the South African War, 1899–1902* (Cambridge, Eng., 1983).

11. Paul Gordon Lauren, *Power and Prejudice: The Politics and Diplomacy of Racial Discrimination* (Boulder, 1988), 63.

12. Ibid., 39.

13. Adas, *Machines as the Measure of Men*, 272–275.

14. On Knox, see Michael Banton, *Racial Theories*, 2d ed. (Cambridge, Eng., 1998), 73–74. On the curious case of Gobineau, whose theoretical racism did not make him an imperialist, a defender of slavery, or even an antisemite, see George L. Mosse, *Toward the Final Solution: A History of European Racism* (Madison, 1985; org. pub. 1978), 51–57. On anti-imperialism among radical racists in the United States, see George M. Fredrickson, *The Black Image in the White Mind: The Debate on Afro-American Character and*

Destiny, 1817–1914 (Middletown, Conn., 1987, orig. pub. 1971), 305–308.

15. Adolf Hitler, *Mein Kampf*, trans. Ralph Manheim (Boston, 1999; orig. pub. 1943), 139.

16. See Cell, *Highest Stage of White Supremacy*; Saul DuBow, *Racial Segregation and the Origins of Apartheid in South Africa, 1919– 1936* (London, 1989); and George M. Fredrickson, *White Supremacy: A Comparative Study in American and South African History* (New York, 1981), chaps. 4–6.

17. C. Vann Woodward, *The Strange Career of Jim Crow*, 3d rev. ed. (New York, 1974), 72–74.

18. See Maurice S. Evans, *Black and White in the Southern States: A Study of the Race Problem in the United States from a South African Point of View* (London, 1915). A new edition of this work with an introduction by George M. Fredrickson was published by the University of South Carolina Press in 2001.

19. See Joel Williamson, *The Crucible of Race: Black-White Relations in the American South since Emancipation* (New York, 1984), 111–223; and Leon F. Litwack, *Trouble in Mind: Black Southerners in the Age of Jim Crow* (New York, 1998), 217–325.

20. Williamson, *Crucible of Race*, 455–458; Fredrickson, *Black Image*, 309–311.

21. Helmut Bley, *South-West Africa under German Rule, 1894– 1914*, trans. Hugh Ridley (Evanston, Ill., 1971), 212–213, 150, 163– 164, 207, and passim (quotations on 164 and 207).

22. Hannah Arendt, *The Origins of Totalitarianism* (New York, 1951), 185–207.

23. Bley, *South-West Africa*, 167–168.

24. Shulamit Volkov, "Antisemitism as a Cultural Code: Reflections on the History and Historiography of Antisemitism in Imperial Germany," *Publications of the Leo Baeck Institute: Year Book XXIII* (London, 1978), 25–46. See also Peter Pulzer, *The Rise of Political Antisemitism in Germany and Austria*, rev. ed. (Cambridge, Mass., 1988, orig. pub. 1964), 185–284.

25. W.E.B. Du Bois, "The African Roots of War," *Atlantic Monthly* 115 (May 1915): 707–714.

26. See Fredrickson, *White Supremacy* chaps. 4–6, and *Black Liberation: A Comparative History of Black ideologies in the United States and South Africa* (New York, 1995), passim.

27. DuBow, *Racial Segregation and the Origins of Apartheid*, 33–38.

28. Gordon A. Craig, *Germany 1866–1945* (New York, 1978), 434–468.

29. Hitler, *Mein Kampf*, 264–329 and passim.

30. Jeffrey Herf, *Reactionary Modernism: Technology, Culture, and Politics in Weimar and the Third Reich* (Cambridge, Eng., 1984).

31. *Mein Kampf*, passim.

32. Ibid., 325.

33. Sander Gilman, *The Jew's Body* (New York, 1991), 76, 188–189, and passim.

34. See Eric Rentschler, *The Ministry of Illusion: Nazi Cinema and Its Afterlife* (Cambridge, Mass., 1996), 149–169.

35. Hitler, *Mein Kampf*, 383.

36. Ibid., 624.

37. Quoted in Benno Müller-Hill, *Murderous Science: Elimination by Scientific Selection of Jews, Gypsies, and Others, Germany, 1933–1945*, trans. George R. Fraser (Oxford, 1988), 86. Müller-Hill uses this statement to raise doubts about Hitler's belief in a biological basis for racism.

38. Alfred Rosenberg, *Race and Race History, and Other Essays*, ed. Robert Pois (New York, 1970), 34, 84.

39. For a recent and controversial presentation of the latter view, see Daniel Jonah Goldhagen, *Hitler's Willing Executioners: Ordinary Germans and the Holocaust* (New York, 1996).

40. Saul Friedlander, *Nazi Germany and the Jews*, vol. 1, *The Years of Persecution, 1933–1939* (New York, 1997), 116.

41. See John Weiss, *Ideology of Death: Why the Holocaust Happened in Germany* (Chicago, 1996).

42. See Stefan Kühl, *The Nazi Connection: Eugenics, American Racism, and German National Socialism* (New York, 1994).

43. Friedlander, *Nazi Germany and the Jews*, 1:142, 149–150.

44. See table 14 in the back of Paul Mendes-Flohr and Jehuda Reinharz, eds., *The Jew in the Modern World: A Documentary History,* 2d ed. (New York, 1995), 714.

45. Friedlander, *Nazi Germany and the Jews,* 1:280–304.

46. See Guenter Lewy, *The Nazi Persecution of the Gypsies* (New York, 2000), 135–148 and passim. Lewy's finding are likely to be controversial, but his study is based on a fuller examination of the sources than previous studies of the Gypsies' experience under Hitler.

47. Friedlander, *Nazi Germany and the Jews,* 1:207–208; Reiner Pommerin, *Sterilisierung der Rheinlandbastarde* (Düsseldorf, 1979).

48. Quoted in John Torpey, " 'Making Whole What Has Been Smashed': Reflections on Reparations," *Journal of Modern History* 73 (2001): 344.

49. Carl N. Degler, *In Search of Human Nature: The Decline and Revival of Darwinism in American Social Thought* (New York, 1991), 203–205. See also Daniel J. Kevles, *In the Name of Eugenics: Genetics and the Use of Human Heredity* (Berkeley, 1986), 251; and Richard A. Soloway, *Demography and Degeneration: Eugenics and the Declining Birthrate in Twentieth-Century Britain* (Chapel Hill, 1990), 353.

50. Quoted in Lauren, *Power and Prejudice,* 136.

51. Gunnar Myrdal, *An American Dilemma* (New York, 1944), 997, lxi.

52. On the effect of the Cold War on American racial thought and policy, see especially Mary L. Dudziak, *Cold War Civil Rights: Race and the Image of American Democracy* (Princeton, 2000).

53. Renee Romano, "No Diplomatic Immunity: African Diplomats, the State Department, and Civil Rights," *Journal of American History* 87 (September 2000): 546–579.

54. See Manning Marable, *Race, Reform, and Rebellion: The Second Reconstruction in Black America, 1945–1990,* 2d ed. (Jackson, Miss., 1991), 13–60.

55. Philip A. Klinkner with Rogers M. Smith, *The Unsteady March: The Rise and Decline of Racial Equality in America* (Chicago, 1999).

56. Lauren, *Power and Prejudice,* 180–186 and passim.

57. See Newel M. Stultz, *Afrikaner Politics in South Africa, 1934–1948* (Berkeley, 1974).

58. See Thomas Borstelmann, *Apartheid's Reluctant Uncle: The United States and Southern Africa in the Early Cold War* (New York, 1993).

59. Quoted in William Henry Vatcher, *White Laager: The Rise of Afrikaner Nationalism* (New York, 1965), 160.

60. Saul DuBow, *Scientific Racism in Modern South Africa* (Cambridge, Eng., 1995), 261–267. On the tension between biological racism and cultural pluralism in Afrikaner nationalist thought during the apartheid era, see also T. Dunbar Moodie, *The Rise of Afrikanerdom: Power, Apartheid, and Afrikaner Civil Religion* (Berkeley, 1975), 259–281.

61. DuBow, *Scientific Racism*, 258. The Tower of Babel legend also provided the scriptural basis for the banning of interracial dating at Bob Jones University in South Carolina, which became an issue in the 2000 political campaign in the United States.

62. Moodie, *Afrikanerdom*, 249.

63. On the history and changing status of the Coloreds of South Africa, see Gavin Lewis, *Between the Wire and the Wall: A History of South African "Coloured" Politics* (New York, 1987), and Fredrickson, *White Supremacy*, chap. 6 and passim.

64. The reasons for the seemingly miraculous fall of apartheid are numerous and complex. For an excellent discussion that acknowledges the end of the Cold War as one of the factors involved, see Hermann Giliomee, "Surrender without Defeat: Afrikaners and the South African 'Miracle,'" *Daedalus* 126 (Spring 1997): 113–145, especially 136 and 139. For my own reflections on the causes of apartheid's demise, see "The Strange Death of Segregation," *New York Review of Books*, May 6, 1999, 36–38.

E P I L O G U E   *Racism at the Dawn of the Twenty-First Century*

1. Donald L. Horowitz, *Ethnic Groups in Conflict* (Berkeley, 1985), 52.

2. George M. Fredrickson, "Understanding Racism" in *The Comparative Imagination: On the History of Racism, Nationalism, and Social Movements* (Berkeley, 1997), 77–97.

NOTES *to Pages 141–163*

3. Horowitz, *Ethnic Groups*, 50.

4. On the "new racism" in the United States and Great Britain, see David Theo Goldberg, *Racist Culture: Philosophy and the Politics of Meaning* (Cambridge, Mass., 1993), 70–89; and Paul Gilroy, "One Nation under a Groove: The Politics of 'Race' and Racism in Britain," in *Anatomy of Racism*, ed. David Theo Goldberg (Minneapolis, 1990), 263–282. French "culturalism" is analyzed in Tzvetan Todorov, *On Human Diversity: Nationalism, Racism, and Exoticism in French Thought*, trans. Catherine Porter (Cambridge, Mass., 1993), 156–157.

5. See George M. Fredrickson, "America's Diversity in Comparative Perspective," *Journal of American History* 85 (1998): 859–875. On "rational discrimination," see Dinesh D'Souza, *The End of Racism: Principles for a Multiracial Society* (New York, 1995), and my review of it in the *New York Review of Books*, October 19, 1995, 10–16.

6. *Regents of the Univ. of Calif. v Bakke*, 438, U.S. 265, 407 (1978).

7. See Bernard Lewis, *Semites and Anti-Semites: An Inquiry into Conflict and Prejudice* (New York: 1999, orig. pub. 1986), 193–272. But Lewis is careful to point out that popular, as opposed to official, antisemitism is not highly developed in the Arab world.

8. On Britain, see Robert Miles, *Racism after "Race Relations"* (London, 1993); and Paul Gilroy, *"There Ain't No Black in the Union Jack": The Cultural Politics of Race and Nation* (Chicago, 1991; orig. pub. 1987). On France, see especially Michel Wieviorka, *La France raciste* (Paris, 1992).

9. See Horowitz, *Ethnic Groups*.

10. Hamish Dickie-Clark, "The Study of Conflict in South Africa and Northern Ireland," *Social Dynamics* 2 (1976): 53–59.

11. Fredrickson, "America's Diversity."

12. See Benjamin R. Barber, *Jihad vs. McWorld: How Globalism and Tribalism Are Reshaping the World* (New York, 1996).

A P P E N D I X   *The Concept of Racism in Historical Discourse*

1. George M. Fredrickson, *White Supremacy: A Comparative Study in American and South African History* (New York, 1981), xii.

2. Loïc J. D. Wacquant, "For an Analytic of Racial Domination," in *Political Power and Social Theory*, vol. 11, ed. Diane E. Davis (Greenwich, Conn., 1997), 222.

3. Kwame Anthony Appiah, "Racisms," in *Anatomy of Racism*, ed. David Theo Goldberg (Minneapolis, 1990), 4–5.

4. See George M. Fredrickson, *The Black Image in the White Mind: The Debate on Afro-American Character and Destiny, 1817–1914* (Middletown, Conn., 1987; orig. pub. 1971), 97–129.

5. I develop this argument in my essay "Understanding Racism," in *The Comparative Imagination: On the History of Racism, Nationalism, and Social Movements* (Berkeley, 1997), 77–97.

6. Zygmunt Bauman, *Modernity and the Holocaust* (Ithaca, 1989), 60–82 (quotation on 60).

7. "Understanding Racism."

8. Théophile Simar, *Étude critique sur la formation de la doctrine des races au XVIIIe siècle et son expansion au XIXe siècle*, Académie Royale le Belgique, *Mémoires*, deuxième série, tome XVI (Brussels, 1922).

9. Ibid., 15–16, 24, 30–33, 64, 75, 109, 215, 229, 283–286, 302–307.

10. See chap. 2 above.

11. Frank H. Hankins, *The Racial Basis of Civilization: A Critique of the Nordic Doctrine* (New York, 1926), ix.

12. Ibid., 89, 93.

13. Ibid., 306–307.

14. Ibid., 343–348.

15. Ibid., 307.

16. Magnus Hirschfeld, *Racism* (Port Washington, N.Y., 1973; orig. pub. 1938).

17. Ibid., 57.

18. Ibid., 228.

19. Ibid., 260.

20. Jacques Barzun, *The French Race* (New York, 1932).

21. This was the original title of the 1937 edition published in New York. It was reprinted with a new introduction but few other

changes in 1965 as *Race: A Study in Superstition* (New York, 1965). Citations are to the 1965 edition.

22. Ibid., xxiii (from the preface to the first edition of 1937).

23. Ibid., 4–5.

24. Ibid., 134.

25. Ibid., 182–183.

26. Ruth Benedict, *Race: Science and Politics* (New York, 1959; orig. pub. 1940), 3–8, 97–139, 146–151 (quotations on 148 and 151).

27. Ibid., 154.

28. Much of this work has been cited elsewhere in this study.

29. Gunnar Myrdal, *An American Dilemma* (New York, 1944). On the impact of Myrdal's study, see especially Walter Jackson, *Gunnar Myrdal and America's Conscience* (Chapel Hill, 1990).

30. Much of this work has also been cited elsewhere in this study.

31. Thomas F. Gossett, *Race: The History of an Idea in America* (Dallas, 1963).

32. George L. Mosse, *Toward the Final Solution: A History of European Racism* (Madison, 1978).

33. Ivan Hannaford, *Race: The History of an Idea in the West* (Baltimore, 1996).

34. Imanuel Geiss, *Geschichte der Rassismus* (Frankfurt am Main, 1988).

INDEX

Adam and Eve story (Genesis), 52, 66
Adas, Michael, 61, 108
affirmative action decision (U.S.), 143
Afghanistan Taliban government, 149
African Americans: affirmative action
and, 143; associated with Southern
defeat, 106; "aversive racism" trig-
gered against, 10; Benedict on equality of, 166; comparison of German
Jews and, 82–85, 86–89, 93–94; competition between immigrants and,
86–87; Curse of Ham associated
with, 29, 43–45, 51–52, 80, 176n.55;
discrimination justified by "dysfunctional" subculture of, 142; emancipation of, 81–84; fear of sexual pollution or violation by, 119–121; French
discussions on ugliness of, 68; Great
Migration to urban North by, 115; intermarriage ban lifted and, 131; Jim
Crow laws and, 83, 101, 102, 109,
110–111, 129, 130, 167; legacy of slavery and perception of, 94–95; post–
World War II racial reform and, 129–
132, 137–138; racial Darwinism and,
85–86; racialism on, 160–161; racism

ideology of inferiority of, 79–81; racist reprisal response to equality of,
93; romantic racialism beliefs about,
154; slavery of, 80–81; voting rights
protection given to, 130; World War
II impact on racial reform and,
129–130. *See also* American white
supremacy
African National Congress, 137
African slavery: Curse of Ham myth justification for, 29, 43–45, 51–52, 80,
176n.55; democratic revolution chal-
lenging, 64–66; lasting legacy of, 94–
95; New World forced labor vs., 38–
40; New World legal/religious status
criteria for, 54–55; origins of race association with, 29–30; precolonial,
30; religious justification of, 38–39;
skin pigmentation as justifying, 39.
See also slavery
Afrikaner nationalism, 3–4
An American Dilemma (Myrdal), 129, 167
American Indians: assimilationism and,
73; assimiliation practiced by tribes
of, 155; bifurcated wild man/noble
savage images of, 36; "black legend"

gimes, 104–105; social construction of racism and, 99–100

Mongolians, 57

Mosse, George, 168

Muslims: Crusade rhetoric and, 19; ethnic differences of Spanish, 40–41; fate of the *Morisco* population of, 34–35; Iberian coexistence of Christians and, 29; modern discrimination against immigrant, 149; purity of blood doctrine and Spanish, 32–34, 35, 40–42; religious basis of Spanish discrimination against, 24–25

Myrdal, Gunnar, 129, 167

Nama genocidal policy, 112

Napoleon, 65, 67, 69

National Association for the Advancement of Colored People, 115

national identity: comparing Spanish and German, 41; formation of Spanish, 40–41; German ethnic criteria for, 69–70; racism and, 75

nationalism: ethnic identification vs. citizenship and, 69–70; *Volkgeister* (national souls), 8, 70, 89, 92, 118, 119, 135–137; *völkisch*, 8

Native Americans. *See* American Indians

"native segregation" (South Africa), 110, 133–134

"A Natural History of Racism" (Benedict), 165

"natural slavery" concept, 36–37

Nazi Germany: antisemitism vitality under, 103; Aryan myth embraced by, 164; examining rise of racist regime in, 105; extreme segregation

practiced in, 2, 123–124, 125–127; Hirschfeld's refutation of doctrines of, 162–163; *Kristallnacht* pogrom of 1938 in, 125; Nuremberg Laws of 1935 in, 2, 123–124, 125, 164–165; as overtly racist regime, 2–3, 101, 123–124; "racial purity" agenda of, 126; World War I defeat and antisemitism of, 106, 107, 162–163. *See also* German Jews; Germany; Hitler, Adolph; Holocaust; overtly racist regimes

Negrophilia: origins of late medieval European, 26–31; Prester John myth, Christianity and, 27–29; U.S. Reconstruction exploitation of, 84

Netanyahu, B., 33

"the new racism," 6–7, 141–142

New World: "black legend" of Spanish in, 41–42; interracial marriage / concubinage of, 39–40, 55; legal / religious status criteria of slavery in, 54–55; Spanish treatment of indigenes in, 35–40. *See also* United States

Nordic superiority theory, 156, 160

Notes on Virginia (Jefferson), 59

Nuremberg Laws of 1935 (Nazi Germany), 2, 123–124, 125, 164–65

Omi, Michael, 75

"the one-drop rule" (American South), 124

On the Natural Varieties of Mankind (Blumenbach), 56

Otherness: conversion to change religious, 44–45, 103, 146–147; domination of white supremacist racism over, 157; fostered image of German Jews, 88–90, 123; as justification for

South-West Africa: German ban on intermarriage in, 102, 112; German genocide policies in, 112–113

Soviet Union, 130, 137

Spain: *caballero* complex of, 42; ethnic differences of Jews/Muslims in, 40–41; fate of the *Morisco* population in, 34–35; formation of national identity in, 40–41; *limpieza de sangre* (purity of blood) doctrine of, 32–34, 35, 40–42, 53; religious basis of discrimination against Muslims in, 24–25; slavery of conquered people policy by, 38; treatment of Jewish converts in, 31–33, 34–35; treatment of New World indigenes by, 35–40

Spanish colonization: "black legend" of, 41–42; interracial marriage/concubinage during, 39–40; treatment of indigenes during, 35–40

Spanish national identity: comparing German and, 41; formation of, 40–41; as *Herrenvolk* egalitarianism basis, 42

Strydom, J. G., 134, 136

supernaturalist racism: Christianity salvation doctrine vs., 46–47; Christian unity of mankind belief vs., 52–54; Curse of Ham myth and, 29, 43–45, 51–52, 80, 176n.55; Jews blamed for Crucifixion and, 18–19, 44, 51

Sweet, James H., 29

Taguieff, Pierre-André, 9

Taliban government (Afghanistan), 149

Thornton, John, 30

Toledo rebellion (1449), 33

Trachtenberg, Joshua, 21

transubstantiation, 20

Treitschke, Heinrich von, 72

UNESCO eugenics statement (1950), 128–129

United Nations: human rights declaration by, 132; South African conference on racism by, 140; on Zionism as racism, 144

United States: abolition of slavery in, 65; adaptation of Jews to modernity of, 94–95; affirmative action in the, 143; ascriptive Americanism nationalism of, 91; assimilationism in, 73–74; church and state separation in, 147–148, 149; Dred Scott decision of 1857 in, 80–81; exclusion and egalitarian norms of, 68–69; impact of World War I on black-white relations in, 115–116; impact of World War II on black-white relations in, 129–130; Jim Crow laws in, 83, 101, 102, 109, 110–111, 129, 130, 137, 167; liberal interracialists of interwar years in, 116; "the new racism" of, 141–142; racial equality fostered by external pressures in, 131–132; racial reform during Cold War in, 129–131, 137–138; racism ideology of black inferiority in, 79–81; Reconstruction period of, 81–84, 106. *See also* American South; New World

universalism: "ascriptive Americanism" challenge to, 91; Enlightenment democratic, 74–75; German reaction against, 69–70; white supremacist racism as distortion of, 91–92

The Unsteady March (Klinkner and Smith), 131

205

ment universalism, 91–92; domination of the Other by, 157; ethnology support of, 57–59; fear of sexual pollution/violation by, 119–121; as justification for colonization, 107–108; as limited description of racism, 155–156; Middle Age origins of, 29–30, 46–47. *See also* American white supremacy; overtly racist regimes; race

Wilberforce, William, 63

"wild men" belief, 35, 36

Williamson, Joel, 110

Winant, Howard, 75

Woodward, C. Vann, 110

World War I: decline of Western imperialism following, 114; impact of defeat on Germany, 106, 118–120, 162–163; impact on U.S./South African black-white relations, 115–117

World War II: focus of German racial ideology during, 165; Holocaust of, 2–3, 92, 100, 121, 127–128, 132; impact on U.S. racial reform by, 129–130; as turning point in racism history, 127

World Wide Web hate sites, 143–144

xenophobia, 6, 140, 146

Zionism, 144